*Discourses delivered to Swamis and Ananda Samajis
of the Nithyananda Order all over the world*

The meditation techniques included in this book are to be practiced only after personal instructions by an ordained teacher of Life Bliss Foundation (LBF). If someone tries these techniques without prior participation in the meditation programs of LBF, they shall be doing so entirely at their own risk; neither the author nor LBF shall be responsible for the consequences of their actions.

Published by Life Bliss Foundation

Copyright© 2009
First Edition: July 2008, 1000 copies
Second Edition: Jan 2009, 2000 copies

ISBN 13: 978-1-60607-015-4   ISBN 10: 1-60607-015-0

All rights reserved. No part of this publication may be reproduced, or stored in a retrieval system, or transmitted in any form or by any means, electronic, mechanical, photocopying, recording or otherwise, without written permission of the publisher. In the event that you use any of the information in this book for yourself, the author and the publisher assume no responsibility for your actions.

All proceeds from the sale of this book go towards supporting charitable activities.

Printed in India by Aditya Printers, Bangalore.
Ph: +91 +80 26606776   mail: prakash@adityaprinters.com

Guaranteed Enlightenment

Ashtavakra Gita

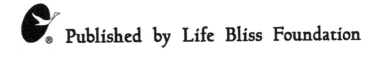 Published by Life Bliss Foundation

Contents

Enlightenment - It is Possible! 7

Enlightenment - Guaranteed!! 55

Enlightenment - Have It!!! 109

Appendix 152

Enlightenment –
It Is Possible!

कथं ज्ञानमवाप्नोति कथं मुक्तिर्भविष्यति ।
वैराग्यं च कथं प्राप्तमेतद्ब्रूहि मम प्रभो ॥

मुक्तिमिच्छसि चेत्तात विषयान् विषवत्त्यज ।
क्षमार्जवदयातोषसत्यं पीयूषवद्भज ॥

न पृथ्वी न जलं नाग्निर्न वायुर्द्यौर्न वा भवान् ।
एषां साक्षिणात्मानं चिद्रूपं विद्धि मुक्तये ॥

यदि देहं पृथक्कृत्य चिति विश्राम्य तिष्ठसि ।
अधुनैव सुखी शान्तो बन्धमुक्तो भविष्यसि ॥

How can knowledge be acquired?
And how can liberation be attained?
And how is renunciation possible?
Tell me this, oh Lord.

If you aspire for liberation my child,
Shun the objects of the senses as poison
And seek forgiveness, sincerity, kindness,
contentment, and truth as nectar.

You are neither earth, nor water, nor fire, nor air, nor ether.
In order to attain liberation realize yourself
as the knower of all these and consciousness itself.

If you detach the body and rest in intelligence,
You will at once be happy, peaceful and free from bondage.

The content of this book was taken from a discourse given by Paramahamsa Nithyananda in Bangalore, India from 10th to 12th of December, 2005.

Introduction

I would like to start with a small story:

> In a school, the boy scouts were supposed to tell their teacher the good deeds that they did for that day. Every day they did some good deeds and came and reported to their teacher. One day three friends stood up and said, 'Sir, today we helped an old lady cross the road.'
>
> The teacher was not able to understand why three students were needed to help an old lady cross the street. He asked the boys, 'Why did you need three people to help an old lady cross the road?'

They said, 'Sir, it took all the three of us because she did not want to cross the road!'

Many times we extend help without thinking about the situation. When we try to help somebody without them seeking help, we create only more and more trouble for them. All our service done out of ego ends up only in creating trouble for others.

I request all of you to ask your doubts and questions. Unless you ask me, I won't be able to help. By you being here, I assume that you are interested or you are asking for help for the ultimate experience of enlightenment. Unless you ask, whatever help I give will only be a problem or trouble for you!

The whole *Ashtavakra Gita*, this great book, was delivered to King Janaka, because Janaka asked for the truth. If you are here just to check out what Nithyananda has got to say, you are welcome. It is not a problem, you are welcome, but please be here completely.

Usually the mind is such that when you get up early in the morning and start brushing your teeth, the mind is already in the office, thinking or worrying about work. When you are actually in the office, your mind is already in the planned evening program, perhaps going to a cinema theatre or temple. When you are sitting in the theater or temple, your mind has already come back to the house.

One thing is sure: if you are here, your mind is not here. Your mind doesn't stay in the same place where your body stays.

Our mind doesn't rest inside our boundary. We all live like ghosts most of the time; our body is in one place, our mind is somewhere else. We don't stay inside our boundary. If you really want this program to help you, if you really want to have some benefit from this program, I request you all to stay inside your boundaries while you are here. Please stay inside your boundary, inside your body. This whole program can do miracles in your being.

Today's subject is 'Enlightenment - It Is Possible!' Before entering into the subject, let me introduce the book, *Ashtavakra Gita*.

Man has created so many spiritual scriptures. But nothing can be compared to *Ashtavakra Gita*. This book is pure spiritual science. It is a technology created by the enlightened Master Ashtavakra, to reproduce the same experience which happened in him.

Understand: a scientist is a person who creates a formula to reproduce things of the outer world. For example, Newton observed something in the outer world and he started contemplating on that experience. He saw an apple falling from the tree and he started contemplating on that experience and created a formula. He created a theory through which people were able to understand gravity.

A scientist creates formulae to reproduce the understanding of the outer world. A spiritual master is a person who creates a formula to reproduce the experience of the inner world.

Ashtavakra is a spiritual scientist. He created a beautiful technology through which he was able to reproduce the same experience that happened in him.

So all you need is just a little sincerity. Just be inside your boundary. You will see that Ashtavakra's *sutras*, his collection of aphorisms, will work miracles on you. The scripture created by him, the technology created by him, can reproduce the same experience which happened in him in you also. All you need to do is, be inside your boundary; be inside your being.

About the boy sage Ashtavakra

The whole story of Ashtavakra is beautiful. We don't know much about Ashtavakra, but there are just a few very significant incidents in his life. The story starts before his birth. It is supposed to be a *puranic* story, an epic story from Hindu mythology. It is very difficult to believe this as a fact.

The story starts when Ashtavakra's mother was carrying him in her womb. Ashtavakra's father used to recite Vedic *mantras*, the chants from the Vedic scriptures. When the father was chanting, the son used to listen to all the *mantras*.

Suddenly, one day the son started questioning the father from inside the womb, 'What you are chanting are pure words. It has no juice; it has no experience. You are just an intellectual *pundit* (learned person). Where is the truth?'

The father was shocked. Ashtavakra was asking, 'What happened to the knowledge? What happened to the wisdom? You are reciting only words. They are just pure words. There is no juice, there is no wisdom in them.' Of course, the father as one can imagine, was hurt.

A *pundit's* ego is always very strong because his whole personality is built on words. Actually we can easily hurt a person who lives with mere words. A pundit can be more easily hurt than anybody else because his whole mind, his whole life is centered on words.

We can easily cheat a pundit. Just give him two or three compliments. Just verbally tell him that he is a great person. He can also easily be hurt by telling him a few words. His whole life is centered on words and more words.

The moment the father was deeply hurt, he cursed the son. He said, 'What! Even before taking birth you dare to question me! Who knows what else you will do after taking birth!' The father's curse resulted in Ashtavakra taking birth with eight problems or deformities in his body. At eight spots, his body was crooked or curved.

I don't know whether this story is a fact or if it really happened. But the story has significance. It has truth in it. Let us understand the truth behind the story. Usually the great masters who take birth on planet Earth take conscious births. Consciously they enter into the mother's womb, enter into the body and start radiating their enlightenment.

The meaning of the story is that Ashtavakra was conscious even before birth. That is the truth. That is the meaning of the story. We cannot prove for sure whether he really spoke or whether he was really cursed. We do not know about this. But the truth which our masters are trying to explain through the story is that Ashtavakra was conscious of his being. He was conscious about his birth.

Now, the next story is another beautiful story:

> Ashtavakra went to the palace of Janaka, a great king. The moment Ashtavakra entered Janaka's palace, everyone in the palace started laughing because Ashtavakra looked ugly with the eight curves in his body. All the ministers and all the people including Janaka started laughing. But Ashtavakra did not get hurt.

If we allow ourselves to become hurt, we are defeated. At any point, if we are hurt, we are defeated. If we become angry, we are defeated.

Ashtavakra was not hurt; he was not disturbed in any way. He was just completely relaxed. He said to Janaka, 'Oh Janaka, I thought you were a great *rishi* (sage). I thought you were a great *yogi* (accomplished spiritual person). But you are neither a *yogi* nor do you have any *yogis* around you. You have only cobblers in your court. You have only shoemakers in your court.'

Ashtavakra boldly says, 'You have only shoemakers in your court.' You need

to understand this statement; it is a beautiful statement. Straightaway, a twelve-year-old boy with physical challenges is talking in a very bold manner to the king of the country.

A twelve-year-old boy, Ashtavakra, has entered the court and the whole court is laughing. If we were in Ashtavakra's place, we would have immediately become angry. First, our ego would have been hurt; it would have been full of anger.

Next, either we would have shouted at the people who laughed or we would have left the place. But here is a person who can never be disrespected in the real sense. Nobody can disrespect a person who lives in spontaneity. Ashtavakra was a spontaneous person with great respect for himself.

Nobody can give us suffering unless we give our silent permission. Unless we allow or give our silent permission, nobody can disrespect us or hurt us.

Ashtavakra was such an integrated being, such a beautiful being, he did not allow others to hurt him or depress him. Straightaway he spoke with spontaneity, 'You have only shoemakers.' Be very clear, if we become angry, we cannot use the right words. But Ashtavakra used the right words: cobblers, shoemakers, etc. Janaka was shocked.

Ashtavakra explains, 'These people are seeing only my skin, not my being. Cobblers see only the skin, not the reality. When the cobbler sees an animal, he will think only about the skin, not the being.'

When a tailor sees you, he will see only your dress. He will measure your being only based on the dress you are wearing. When a jeweler sees you, he will first see only the jewelry you are wearing. He will judge you based on the jewelry that you are wearing. He weighs you based on the gold that you are wearing.

People look at things only from their angles. They have their own ideas; they have their own imagination.

> Ashtavakra says, 'You have only cobblers around you - people who only see the skin, not the being. My body has eight curves, no doubt. But my being is pure; my being is straight.'

You can't upset a man who lives in spontaneity. You can't stop him; you can't disrespect him.

There is a beautiful Zen story:

> A well-known Zen master was giving a beautiful discourse. A Buddhist monk, a learned person who was well read but had not experienced anything, came to this discourse. The moment he entered the hall, he started shouting. 'What Zen do you know? What spirituality do you know? What are you talking about?'
>
> The Zen master was a young person. The learned man kept on shouting, 'What are you talking about, what Zen do you know? You can make only these fools listen to what you say. You can't make me listen to you. Can you make me listen to what you say?'
>
> The Master was very polite. He just said, 'Sir can you please come closer? I am not able to hear you properly.'
>
> The monk came with all his arrogance. Then the master said, 'Can you please come this side?' The monk went to the side.
>
> Then the master turned his face, 'I am still not able to hear you properly. Can you move a little closer to the other side please?' The monk moved a little closer to the other side.
>
> Then the master said, 'You seem to be a nice person. You have already listened

to what I said three times. Now please sit down and listen to the rest of the discourse!'

The Zen master was spontaneous here! A person who lives in spontaneity can never be disrespected. We can never catch him.

Ashtavakra was a person who lived in spontaneity. He lived completely in the present moment. He could neither be disrespected nor be deluded by the ego. He was not disturbed. He was just clear about his being. He said clearly, 'Janaka, you have only cobblers around you.' These words really touched Janaka. He understood these words.

Janaka was an intelligent king, a rare politician and a rare being. Being a king and having intelligence is something quite unique. Janaka was a king and an intelligent being. He understood the meaning of the words spoken by Ashtavakra.

He immediately came down from the throne, touched the feet of Ashtavakra and said, 'Please forgive me. I understand what you say.' Not only did he ask Ashtavakra to forgive him, but he also put forth one more statement. 'Master, oh Lord...' - he called Ashtavakra as Master. Janaka continued, 'Oh Lord, just from your very words, I understood that what you spoke was from your own direct experience.'

Please understand, if you want to find out whether somebody is enlightened or just an intellectual *pundit*, observe him when he is hurt, or when he is disrespected. See how he behaves when he is disrespected. That will clearly show whether he has experienced the Truth or he is just an intellectual pundit.

We can have our titles or position or status. We can keep everything as long as our ego is not hurt. The moment our ego is hurt, the septic matter, the pus that is inside the infected wound will come out. If we have ego, the pus will simply come out. We will radiate anger, violence and vengeance.

How a person behaves and how he responds when he is hurt or when he is disrespected, will give you clarity as to whether he is really enlightened or whether he is just an intellectual pundit.

Here, Ashtavakra was completely disrespected. If you say a word and then laugh at someone, the other person will not be hurt so much. But if you just look at them and laugh, their very being is rejected. When you enter someone's house, if you start to speak and if people start laughing and talking, then you can understand that they are not ready to hear what you have to say. However, if they start laughing the moment you enter, your very being is not being accepted.

Here, the very being of Ashtavakra was rejected and disrespected by the ministers of the court. But he was not offended; he was not disturbed. When you address the Masters you cannot use the word 'was'; we can only use the word 'is'. We can't use the past tense 'was' for them. We can't say 'He was'; we can only say 'He is'. When we mention the incidents of the past, we have to use the word 'was' to be grammatically correct. However, when we speak about the Masters, they 'are'. They are always available; they are in the present.

You see, dead masters are not absent as you think they are. Moreover, the living masters are not present as you think they are. It is their energy, sheer presence that gives them the authority.

Ashtavakra was not hurt because he was so clear about his being and he was clearly expressing the reality. Janaka then said, 'Just by your few words, I can understand that you are an enlightened being. Your words are from your very being. Please teach me. Please give me the wisdom that you have.'

Because Janaka asked for the truth, whatever Ashtavakra taught became a big help to him. It helped King Janaka to transform his life, to awaken his being, to achieve enlightenment.

Unless you ask for this help, it cannot be given. If I give it to you without you asking, it will be just like the scout boys helping the old lady to cross the road. Three boys had to help one lady because she did not want to cross the road.

So please be very clear, I do not want to force the help on you. By you being here, I assume you are requesting this help. So I am entering into the *sutra,* the aphorism.

Janaka's Enquiries into the Truth

I am entering into the *Ashtavakra Gita,* assuming you need the wisdom and knowledge of Ashtavakra.

Let me give the *slokas* (verses) in English itself and then I will give the explanation.

Janaka asked:
How can knowledge be acquired?
And how can liberation be attained?
And how is renunciation possible?
Tell me this, oh Lord.

It is a beautiful question. Janaka's very being is a seeker. He might have laughed at Ashtravakra by mistake, but his very being is a seeker. He is a seeker of the truth, of reality. So he is asking:

How can knowledge be acquired? How is liberation attained?

How is renunciation possible? Tell me this oh Lord.

We need to understand the word 'liberation'.

Liberation means not being disturbed, polluted or touched by the inner or outer world goals. If we are not touched, polluted or corrupted by the outer world or inner world goals, we are liberated.

The Purposelessness of Life

The moment we understand the purposelessness of the whole Existence, we are liberated. I am using a big word here, 'purposelessness'.

Whatever we think as purpose binds our lives. Bondage is thinking that there is a purpose in our lives.

Immediately you may ask the next question, 'What do you mean Master? Is there no purpose in our lives?' Your life has meaning, but it has no purpose. Be very clear, purpose means that we are constantly worried about the goal. We are constantly bothered about what has to be achieved.

Be very clear:

A goal is not the result of life. Life itself is the goal of life.

For example, in one month if we earn 1000 dollars, we measure our thirty days time as 1000 dollars. Mentally, by and by we start calculating the value of a month of our life as equal to 1000 dollars. Whenever we go to a store, we measure in our mind, 'Oh, to buy this dress, I have to work 15 days', 'To buy this jewelry, I have to work two months'.

We measure how much a month of our life is worth based on money. Be very clear, if someone says that he will give you 100 years' salary in a lump sum if you are willing to die today, would you accept it? No! But our mind has been conditioned so much, we measure our whole life based on the money which we earn each month.

The value of our life is calculated by our mind based on the money that we make. We need to understand one important thing, our life is not equal to the money or wealth which we are creating. Money or wealth is beautiful as long as we use it properly.

Be very clear, when we start measuring our whole life just based on money, when our

whole life is centered only on money, we are seriously missing something in life. Something is seriously wrong with our thinking system.

When we start measuring our life based on the money that we make, we are living in a miserable condition. If we measure our whole life just based on the money we are making, we will be happy only on the first and the second day of the month when we receive our salary. The next twenty-eight days of the month we will be waiting just for those two paydays. We will be selling our twenty-eight days just to be happy on those two days. Please do not sell your life. Do not sell your life for some goals.

Two things: First, if we sell our life for some goal, we may not achieve anything at all and feel frustrated. Second, we may achieve our goal, but still feel depressed.

Be very clear, there is an important phrase that needs to be understood: 'depression of success' or the depression *induced by* success. Depression which happens after failure is not real depression because there is always somebody who can give you hope that you will be successful the next time. If we face the depression out of failure, we always have some hope that somebody can inspire us to run again. But if we face the depression after success, nothing can be done. If you are an intelligent person, around the age of forty to forty-five, you have to face the depression of success. This is the scale to find out whether you are intelligent or not. If you are forty to forty-five and you still have not faced the depression of success, be very clear something is seriously wrong and missing in your life.

Around the age of forty to forty-five, you have to face the depression of success because around that age you would have achieved whatever you wanted to achieve. But suddenly you realize, 'I have achieved whatever I wanted to achieve, but I have not satisfied the original reason that created the very desire for that particular achievement.'

Achieving 'what you want' is different from satisfying 'why you wanted it'.

You always wanted the house, car, relationships and bank balance for the sake of a happy life. But by the time you achieve all these things, you are conditioned to suffer. The concept of liberation means understanding the pure purposelessness of life.

In your young age when you are happy and blissful by nature, when you are bubbling and overflowing with energy, you postpone your joy. You always have some purpose, some goal in front of you.

When in college, you tell yourself, 'After graduating from college, I think I will relax and then I will be happy.' After finishing college you think, 'Once I get a job and settle down, then I'll be peaceful.' Once you get the job, you push your happiness further, 'I think after my marriage I'll be happy and blissful.' Once married, you think, 'Once my kids are born, I'll be happy.' After the kids you think, 'Once they all grow up and finish their education, I think I'll be happy.' By the time they are settled in their life, you are conditioned to suffer.

The stress of suffering or worrying becomes part of your being. You are completely conditioned to suffer. After that, if the worry or stress is taken away from you, you feel lonely. You feel you are missing something. You feel that you are not as you were earlier in life. That is the reason elderly people cannot sit with themselves. They get hold of somebody and start talking to them.

It is not accidental that all around the world, all grandparents tell stories to their grandchildren. This is the tradition not only in Indian culture, but all around the world in all cultures. This tradition started not for the sake of children but for the sake of the grandparents because they feel lonely.

We can see this in our lives. There are elderly people who have been married, their children

have also been married, and sometimes even their grandchildren may have been married. Despite this, they will continue to sit and read the matrimonial column in the newspaper with big glasses! They cannot sit with themselves. They cannot relax with themselves. Relaxing within ourselves is what I call liberation.

A person who can sit with himself without expecting anything from the outer world is liberated. He is *jeevan mukta* or liberated soul. Don't think of complicated meanings for the word *jeevan mukta*. If you have a big ideology about *jeevan mukta*, you will never think it is possible to attain.

Today's subject is 'Enlightenment - It is possible!' You will never understand that it is possible, if you associate it with complex ideologies. Understand, it is very simple. The actual definition is...

***Jeevan mukta* means, 'A person who can sit with himself, one who doesn't need anything from the outer world to entertain him, excite him and make him peaceful or happy.'**

Liberation means understanding the purposelessness of life. It means understanding clearly that our lives cannot be measured by the money that we make. Life is something which is more than the money we make. It is not the 1000 dollars per month that we make. If we think that 1000 dollars is our life, we will live in hell for twenty eight days of the month and be in heaven only for the two days of salary. We will be selling twenty eight days of our lives each month for these two days.

A person who keeps money or other things as his goal will be happy and blissful only for those few moments when he achieves his goal. When we understand that whatever goals we may have achieved, nothing in life has a purpose and life itself has no separate purpose, we will start living from moment to moment. We will respect every moment. We will start respecting life itself. We will start living in the present.

When we drop the goal from our mind, our very work will become beautiful and joyful. We will not be running for something. The very running will be beautiful.

If we are thinking of a goal while running, we will never see the beautiful garden that is around us. If we are just running for the sake of pleasure, we will enjoy the garden and we will reach the goal. Both will happen.

Infuse a little bit of peace and bliss in your life and you will understand the purposelessness of life. If you think life has a purpose, you will never understand the meaning of life.

The moment you understand that life has no purpose, that moment you will be liberated. That moment you will understand the meaning of life - living in this moment.

Krishna says:
'*Karmanye vaadhikaaraste maa phaleshu kadaachana*'

You have a right only to work, but never to its outcome. It means, do not live a goal-oriented life and do not think life has a purpose.

The Wave in the Ocean

Understand that our whole life is just a small wave in the ocean of the cosmic energy. In this vast cosmic energy, in this cosmos, in this *Brahmaanda*, in the universal energy, we are just a small wave.

Suddenly the wave thinks, 'Oh, I should protect myself,' and starts asking the neighboring waves, 'Please be my wife,' 'Please be my husband' or 'Please be my son.' It starts asking these waves, 'Let us all protect ourselves, let us all live together and let us all live a happy life.' Then the wave collects a few grains of sand from the beach and says, 'This is my treasure.'

The wave starts thinking this is the purpose of life. With the neighboring waves

supporting it, it thinks it is protected. It locks two or three sand grains and two or three pebbles with another wave and says, 'See, I am lending all this money to you. You have to give it back when I ask.' And the wave thinks it is completely secure and protected. But it doesn't understand that the next moment it is going to disappear into the same ocean!

We are all like the waves. It is all just a few minutes of drama. The next moment we are going to disappear into the same ocean!

Just like how the wave thinks it is separate from the ocean and wants to protect itself and starts collecting a few pebbles from the beach and thinks it is rich or it is secure with life insurance, we also do the same thing.

Life insurance is another big drama. You cannot use the word 'life insurance' at all. It should actually be 'death insurance'! See, after you die, your family, friends or relatives get that money which they have been waiting for.

So you cannot call it life insurance; you can only call it death insurance.

So be very clear, just like how the wave thinks that it is secure by collecting a few pebbles, in the same way we also think that we are safe by having a few diamonds in our safe deposit box.

Those pebbles and our diamonds are one and the same. Diamonds have market value because people want to possess these rare stones. It is only because of the foolish desires of the few people who want to possess this stone that the market value exists. Otherwise, an ordinary stone and a diamond are one and the same. That stone and this stone are one and the same. A diamond has market value because people are competing to possess it.

No stone can protect us. Just as the wave thinks that by collecting a few pebbles it is protected, its life is insured, it is secure, we also think that possessing few things is what makes us secure. Life is pure purposelessness.

Even though it is slightly difficult to understand this truth because of our social conditioning, the moment we understand it, we will be liberated.

A person who understands that life has no purpose will start working ten times more intensely than others. Do not think you will become lazy when you realize that life is without purpose.

Liberation Naturally Leads to Creativity

People always ask me, 'Master, you say life is purposeless. When we start thinking about this, we don't want to work, what should we do now?' Understand this: because we have created too many negative thoughts about our work, because we are conditioned to think of work as punishment or hell, the work creates stress. Because we are again and again conditioned with these ideas, the moment we understand that life is purposeless, we want to escape from work. It is only because of our conditioning, not because of our understanding.

Now if we really understand that life has no purpose, the stress and peer pressure to achieve success will be removed from us. The moment the peer pressure is removed from our being, we will be liberated. And I tell you, a liberated person will be much more creative!

A liberated person will be energetic. A liberated person, by his own understanding, will start actually working.

Understanding life's purposelessness will not lead us to laziness. If it is leading us to laziness, be very clear, we have a negative attitude towards our work. We have already built up a negative attitude towards our work. That is the reason we try to escape the moment we obtain this understanding.

But if we sincerely understand the beauty of purposelessness, if we understand that life is without purpose, we will be continuously

working without stress, without the pressure of the goal, without constantly thinking about the goal.

See, two kinds of societies have been created. One kind believes that man can be made to work only if he is run by fear and greed. He can be enslaved only if he is constantly taught that he is not enough. The other group believes that man will express his energy totally if he is already fulfilled.

The eastern *rishis* believe that man will express his energy to the maximum if he believes that he is already full. That is the first truth you are taught in Eastern mysticism by the mystics - you are full.

When the Whole is removed from the Whole, the Whole remains as the Whole.

Running Driven by Fear and Greed

In the Eastern mystical tradition, you are asked to express yourself just out of your fullness. You are not made to run based on fear and greed. Some other social systems believe that man will work only out of fear and greed. This is why you are taught in your colleges and universities that you are not full, that life has some utility.

Understand that life has no utility. If you believe that life has some utility value, you will constantly be hypnotized into thinking that you are not enough unto yourself. Constantly you are taught that you are not enough. But with the eastern *rishis*, you are constantly taught that you are enough unto yourself. With this very idea, you can enjoy life. Life is to be lived joyfully with a fullness, not with a feeling of inadequacy.

If we understand that we are full and express our fullness, we will also become compassionate. We will attract more and more joyful things and experiences in our life. If we believe strongly that we are not enough unto ourselves and start running based on fear and greed, we will only create and attract incidents and people of the same

nature. By our very nature, we will reproduce what we believe.

If anything has to survive, it should reproduce itself. If we believe our life has to be driven by fear and greed, we will reproduce that same thing in everybody. We will reproduce that same fear and greed in everyone in our life.

Children are told, 'Do this and I will give you candy. If you don't do this I will punish you.' If a small child is managed based on fear and greed, it is acceptable. But, after we are 80, if we still need to be handled with fear and greed, it means we are mentally retarded! Clearly, we have not grown! A child can be handled with fear and greed, but WE don't need fear and greed. When you ask the question, 'What is the benefit of this action?' you are actually asking based on fear and greed.

If you compare the crime rate, incidents of depression, etc. between the societies which are based on the attitude 'enough' and the societies which are based on the attitudes of 'more and more' or 'what next, what next', you will see a big difference and will understand what fear and greed can do to you.

In the Indian society, the civilization is the outcome of 10,000 years of research and development, by at least one billion inner scientists who were working with human consciousness in at least one million inner science laboratories. When I say inner science laboratories, I mean all the temples and ashrams. In India, there are one million temples and ashrams where congregation happens every day. People gather daily in at least one million inner science laboratories - temples and ashrams. The societal systems that are developed based upon the modern science and intellect, which are hardly five hundred years old, are based on the idea that we know everything and we can solve everything. People have started questioning that kind of civilization because it does not have answers for their basic problems.

The problem with the intellect is that it continuously divides. Whereas the quality of emotion is that it always unites. The society that is based on the idea that we know everything or we can solve everything holds the theory that our intellect is the ultimate. These societies have started facing terrible failures.

Constantly running after something puts tremendous pressure on a person. If we understand that life is purposeless, we will realize the futility of constantly running after some goal. The pressure of running after the goal and the stress that comes out of it will simply drop.

Because of running behind goals, we have a split personality. One half of our being is thinking about the goal, the other half of our being is thinking about the path. The moment we understand that the goal is useless, we will be integrated and we will be on the path. The very path, the very life becomes liberation.

Working out of liberation is what I call working as an enlightened being, an enlightened CEO! If you are working out of liberated consciousness, you live in leader consciousness. You achieve the state of the leader.

The status of the leader is different from state of the leader. The status of the leader relates to our society, our position, our bank balances, etc. The state of the leader relates to our understanding of life. If we have this deep understanding, we will achieve the state of the leader, the 'leader consciousness'. Man will be liberated only if he lives in leader consciousness.

'Should I Renounce?'

Janaka asks:
How to achieve liberation?
How is renunciation possible?
Tell me this, Oh Lord.

Renunciation is a beautiful word. People always come and ask me, 'Master, should I renounce everything to achieve enlightenment? Should I renounce everything to realize the Divine?'

I tell them, 'No, just renounce what you don't have, that is enough.'

You don't have to renounce what you have, just renounce what you don't have.

Fear, anxiety, unnecessary worries, unnecessary fantasies, excessive imagination - all these things are not really there in your real life. However, mentally you are living with all these things.

Ninety nine percent of your worries never come true. The one percent that does come true is always good for you.

Fear itself is nothing but negative fantasy. You are living with so many things that you do not really have. Just live with whatever you have and renounce what you do not have, that is enough. All these things exist only in the mind, not in reality. If you do not have Ms. Universe as your wife, but mentally, you have a greed for it, renounce it, that's all! That is what I mean when I say, renounce what you don't have. Then you can live peacefully with what you have!

Entering into *Ashtavakra Gita*

Now, let us give our prayers to Ashtavakra, the great enlightened master, to help us understand the technology created by him, the formula created by him, so we may achieve the same state of Ashtavakra, the same state of enlightenment.

Please close your eyes and pray to that ultimate energy that gave this science to all of us through Ashtavakra. Pray to Him intensely. Let Him give us a deep

understanding about this science, let Him help us understand this science, let this become our experience and let this become part of our being. Let us digest the teachings and the technology of Ashtavakra.

Ashtavakra starts the beautiful answer:

> If you aspire for liberation my child, shun the objects of the senses as poison and seek forgiveness, sincerity, kindness, contentment, and truth as nectar.
>
> You are neither earth, nor water, nor fire, nor air, nor ether.
> In order to attain liberation realize yourself as the knower of all these and consciousness itself.

These two *slokas* (verses), *sutras* (techniques) are beautiful. In the first *sutra*, he speaks about a few things, a few qualities - the basic qualities like shunning the objects of the senses, seeking forgiveness, being sincere, being kind, being content and living with the truth. In the second *sutra*, he expresses the technology. He says that *you are neither earth, nor water, nor fire, nor air or ether. In order to attain liberation, realize yourself as the knower of all these and consciousness itself.* It is a beautiful verse.

In the first part he gives a few disciplines, a few moral lessons. In the second part he gives the technology to achieve the state. This is the way they presented in those days. First, a little bit of discipline, then enlightenment! But I tell you, for modern men, unless the experience itself happens, we can't even ask him to be disciplined. If you tell him, 'Please shun the objects of the senses,' he will ask, 'What for? Why? What is the need? We are very happy. Why should we do all these things?'

Unless we can give one the direct experience, we cannot tell modern man anything. We cannot give him all this advice. Advice is one thing that everybody gives and nobody takes! With modern man we cannot say, 'First enter into all this, then you can experience.' This is the reason why our spirituality is outdated.

In the modern day, we will have to put the second *sutra* first and the first *sutra* second.

Only after our experience, extraordinary discipline will follow in our lives. We cannot force discipline on anyone. We can only work towards the alchemy, the transformation of our being. We can only work towards enlightenment. Once that experience starts happening, automatically the morality will happen to us; the discipline will happen in us.

So I am explaining the second *sutra* first. Let us enter into the second *sutra* first. Then the first *sutra* will simply start happening in our lives.

Life is not a chain. Every moment is independent.

We are neither earth, nor water, nor fire, nor air or ether.

In order to attain liberation, realize yourself as the knower of all these and consciousness itself.

You think about your life either in a positive way or in a negative way. You think of your life as a chain of beautiful incidents or you think of your life as a chain of many sufferings. Usually you think it is only a chain of suffering. Whether you think of it as a chain of suffering, or as a chain of beautiful incidents, both are just expressing your ignorance.

Be very clear, your life is not an interconnected chain as you think it is. Every moment is individual; every moment is a separate, independent moment.

We are just 'un-clutched' beings. Because you are usually clutched, you think it is a single

chain. Because you never un-clutched, you think that you are an interconnected chain. Be very clear, any moment you can just un-clutch yourself. Any moment you can liberate yourself.

Here Ashtavakra says:
We are neither earth, nor water, nor fire, nor air, nor ether.

Whether he is actually requesting you to believe this statement or not, I do not know; but I am not requesting you to believe this. Let me be very clear, I am not asking you to believe that you are *neither earth, nor water, nor fire, nor air, nor ether.* I am just stating the fact that you are *neither earth, nor water, nor fire, nor air, nor ether.* I am just expressing the truth. If you are intelligent enough, it will resonate in your being and you will feel connected to what I am saying. You will feel the truth of my words deeply. If it happens in you, come tomorrow. Otherwise, relax.

All these truths cannot be imbibed by simply believing. I only request that you just be completely present here and try to listen to whatever is being stated and try it in your life. If you are a seeker or if you are going to be helped by these scriptures or by me, these words will simply start creating a new healing effect inside your being. You will experience a deep inner healing.

A feeling of connection will happen. You will start feeling that you are connected deeply with the Truth. If that feeling happens, be very clear, you are ready for the experience. You are ready to experience. We cannot prove or analyze all these statements with logic. These statements are not intended to be proved logically.

Significance of *Ashtavakra Gita* in Vivekananda's life

A beautiful incident occurred:

Vivekananda asks Ramakrishna, 'Master, why don't you prove God logically?'

Ramakrishna laughs and replies, 'If I prove God logically, logic will become God. Logic will be raised to a level higher than God Himself. God is at a higher level. God is great because He can't even be proved by logic.'

Ramakrishna then gives the same *Ashtavakra* book to Vivekananda and asks him to read it. But Vivekananda was completely confused and depressed at that time. He says, 'Why should I read all these things? I don't want to.'

But Ramakrishna says, 'I am not asking you to read it for yourself. Please read it for my sake. I am old, I can't read. You are young, your eyes are fresh. Just read it for my sake so that I can listen. Just read a few lines.'

And the story says that Vivekananda was able to read only a few *sutras*. The very *sutra* started shaking him. He started shivering. He started trembling and tears started flowing. He just dropped the book and started begging Ramakrishna, 'I don't know why but I can't read this book anymore. My whole being is shaken.'

No Need to Believe - Just Listen!

Be very clear, if you listen intensely, your whole being will be shaken. If you are shaken, this book is for you, I am for you. If it doesn't happen, do not worry. There are so many other beautiful programs. Use your time in a much better way.

When you work with the truth, you do not need to believe it. The very power of the truth will shake you.

The very power of the truth will start working in you. You will not be able to forget the very power of the truth.

People ask me, 'Master, how do we remember all your teachings and follow them in our lives?'

I tell them, 'Never make that mistake. Never try to remember my teachings. If my teachings are the truth, you will not have to remember them. *They* will remember *you*! Just listen and understand. Whenever it is necessary they will automatically come up and make you act according to the truth.'

If you have to force yourself to think, remember and then practice, then it is not truth. Truth needs no belief.

Here Ashtavakra is declaring:
You are neither earth, nor water, nor air, nor fire nor ether.
In order to attain liberation, realize your self as the knower of all these and consciousness itself.

He says that you are neither body nor mind nor any of these five elements. Your body and mind are created out of these five elements. You are filled with earth, water, fire, air and ether —your thoughts are comprised of ether. You are filled with all these elements, but you are not these elements. You are beyond them all. Understand yourself as pure consciousness. Realize that you are the knower of these elements and that you are consciousness itself.

You are Not the Body; You are Not the Mind

You do not have to think that you are the body to be alive. Be very clear, you do not have to think you are the mind to think.

Someone approached Ramana Maharshi and said, '*Bhagavan*, six rupees (a few cents) is more than enough to live in Tiruvannamalai for one month.' Ramana's ashram is located here. In those days, the cost of living was very low.

Bhagavan replies, 'To live, even body and mind are not necessary. Why do you need six rupees?'

Understand, even our body and mind are not necessary to live. When we understand that we are beyond our body, our body becomes graceful. When we understand that we are beyond our mind, our mind becomes intelligent. We start radiating grace and intelligence when we understand that we are beyond body and mind.

There is a beautiful *sutra* in Ayurveda where healing and spirituality are explained beautifully. In India, everything, whether it is art, culture, painting, festival, medicines, clothes or anything else, is connected to spirituality. Spirituality is the backbone of India.

The Ayurvedic science says, we get stomach problems like constipation, etc. only if we are constantly holding on to our body. If we can just relax and witness, if we start understanding that we are not the body, we will never have stomach problems.

If anyone of you has a stomach problem try the following technique, it is very effective. In the last two and a half years, I have met more than a million people. One million people have tried the meditation techniques and technologies created by me and experienced the truth or bliss in their lives.

I tell you from my experience, if you have stomach problems, try the following technique for just two to three days. Constantly think that you are not the body. I assure you, you will be liberated from the stomach problem. Your stomach will simply be healed.

One more thing: I am not giving you false hopes or statements. After the experience of two and half years and after working with one million people, I am giving this statement. After thousands of case studies, I am making this statement. After long research I am telling

you that if you have stomach problems including ulcer, constipation, irritation, any problem related to the stomach, this technique will help you. For two or three days, just continuously think, 'I am not the body,' 'I am not the body.' Just relax and allow the body to function. I tell you, within two or three days you will be healed.

The moment we start thinking that we are the body, we begin suffocating the body, we start forcing the body, we start abusing the body. We start disrespecting the body. When we think we are the body, we start disrespecting and abusing it.

You can see in your own lives that you destroy your body for the sake of your enjoyments. You will sit and watch a cricket game on television until midnight even when you are tired. Your eyes will be burning and begging you for a little rest. During the commercial breaks your eyes close automatically; but you tell yourself, 'No, this is not the time for me to sleep.' When the commercial ends, you start watching the television again. You are abusing your eyes for the sake of your pleasure.

We abuse and disrespect our body for our ego satisfaction. The moment that we start realizing that we are not the body, we allow the body to function as it is. We allow the body to function naturally.

By its very nature, the body heals itself. The body has its own intelligence.

Never think that our body is healthy because of us. It is healthy in spite of us. It is healthy not because of us, but in spite of us.

You are constantly abusing and torturing your body. The moment you start thinking, 'I am the body,' you start abusing the body. If you can relax from the idea that you are the body, you will start respecting the body. You will allow the body to live as it wants. You will allow the body intelligence to function. You will allow the body to live naturally. You will not interfere with your body. You will be alive, bubbling and overflowing with energy. You will radiate grace.

The moment you start understanding that you are not the mind, you will have sharp intelligence and spontaneity. You can see this in your own life. If two people are playing a game of chess and if you are watching the game, you will know better moves than the two players. If you are playing, those moves might not be so obvious to you. If you are just watching you will tell them, 'Hey, why don't you do this? Why don't you do that?' But if you yourself are playing, you will not be able to do that.

Just the pressure to win makes you dull. When you are witnessing, when you are away, you don't have the pressure to win. When the pressure to win is not there you become so intelligent, so spontaneous and so alive. Your mind starts radiating intelligence.

When Ashtavakra says,

You are not the body, you are not the mind
You are not the earth, you are not the water,

You are not the fire, you are not the air,

You are not the ether

He says that you are not the five elements. We always think we are the body and mind which is made out of the five elements.

First thing, understand that you are not this body and mind. When you understand that you are not this body and mind, you will start respecting the body and mind. You will start living with your body and mind blissfully. You will not abuse your body. You will not disrespect your body intelligence. You will let your body live naturally and blissfully.

The *Sutra* to Freedom - Detach from the Body and Rest in Intelligence

The next *sutra*:
If you detach from the body and rest in intelligence,
You will at once be happy, peaceful and free from bondage.

I think in these one or two *sutras*, Ashtavakra completely expresses whatever he wants to say. Usually, intelligence is required to explain things in a clear manner. To understand these Truths from just two or three statements also requires intelligence.

A small story:

> A man from Texas goes to a European country. There he meets a farmer. The European farmer starts speaking about his farming, agriculture, and all his activities.
>
> The Texan asks, 'Where is your farm? Can you please show me?'
>
> The European farmer says, 'I have ten acres in front of my house and twenty acres to the side of my house.'
>
> The European farmer was very proud of his thirty-acre land. He asks the Texan, 'How many acres of land do you own? How do you do agriculture?'
>
> The Texan says, 'How many acres? I don't know. Early in the morning, I start travelling in my car and it goes on and on and on. I can reach the other side of the boundary only by evening.'
>
> The European farmer immediately says, 'Oh, is that so? A long time ago, I too had a car like that!'

Please understand, the Texan says that he has a large piece of land. But the European farmer thinks that he is talking about his car moving very slowly. You speak from one angle and the person understands from another angle.

You need intelligence to present something in just a few words. In the same way, you also need intelligence to understand something in a few words.

Bernard Shaw wrote a forty-page book and then made a statement, 'I didn't have enough time. If I had enough time, I would have used my intelligence and reduced the contents to twenty pages. Because I didn't have enough time, I wrote a forty-page book.'

Be very clear, do not think if the book is voluminous, it contains intelligence. Many times a few *sutras*, one or two lines will give the whole clarity. It can transform your whole life.

In today's discourse, I want to express one simple thing: the concept that there is something called enlightenment and that it is possible. There is something called living in the body and mind without being touched by the body and mind. If we can live inside the body and mind without being touched by the body and mind, we can live a liberated life.

If you understand the technology given to us by Ashtavakra, it is not only possible, it is also guaranteed. If you have the courage to enter into the technology of Ashtavakra, you can just have it. Today I say it is possible. Tomorrow, I will explain how it is guaranteed, and the day after tomorrow, you should just have it! There is nothing else that needs to be done.

Now all you need to understand is two simple things.

First, you are not the body and mind.

Second, if you detach from the body and rest in intelligence, you will at once be happy, peaceful and free from bondage.

You will immediately become peaceful the very moment you understand that you are not the body or the mind. Tremendous peace will start happening in you. You will start understanding and accepting yourself as you are. In that very moment, you will start relaxing into yourself. In that very moment, you will become silent. That very moment will bring bliss in you.

The moment you understand that you are not the body and mind, you will relax from this whole *samsara sagara*, ocean of material existence. As long as you continue to associate yourself with the body and mind, you will experience all the sufferings and pains of the body and mind.

Ego is Not Necessary

Just understand this simple thing: in order for an animal such as a cow to breathe, it does not need ego, it does not need an identity and it does not need any character. But you are afraid that if you drop your identity you will not be able to use your body. You are afraid if you drop your identity, your body will not function smoothly. You have an idea about yourself, 'I am somebody's father', 'I am somebody's brother', 'I am somebody's son' and so on. This idea that you have, this identity that you carry, this ego that you carry, is not necessary for the smooth functioning of your body and mind. Of course it is very difficult to believe this.

A small story:

> A person who was born blind went to a doctor and asked the doctor, 'Please do something and give me eyesight.' The doctor said, 'I will perform a surgery and you will be able to see. Then you will be able to walk without the help of the walking stick.'
>
> The blind man said, 'Doctor, I understand you will perform a surgery. I understand that I will get my eyesight. But I am not able to understand how I can walk without my stick!'

We cannot convince the blind man that he can walk without the stick after the surgery. We cannot convince him intellectually because over time he has started associating his walking itself with the stick. Only after the surgery can he understand that he can walk without the stick. Once he gets his eyesight, he will throw away the stick and walk.

Similarly, you do not need your ego to live in the body and mind. Just like how the blind person could not understand that he would be able to walk without the stick after the surgery, you are not able to understand that you can also live in the body and mind without the ego. You can live inside your body, inside your mind without the ego. Just as the blind man who had gained his vision does not need the stick to walk, you do not need the ego to live.

The ego, the concept that you have about you, and the personality that you are carrying, are not necessary for you to live inside the body and mind.

You are afraid that if you drop that personality, people may cheat and exploit you. You fear that you may be taken for a ride and somebody may cheat you in your business. Somebody may take away all your property. You are concerned that if you feel that you are not the body, you will not maintain your house, you may give it away. Please be very clear, all these fears are created in you only by your ego.

Ego uses Fear to Exploit You

As long as you are afraid, you can be exploited by the ego.

Whoever wants to exploit you, the first thing they have to do is to create fear in you. If someone wants to exploit you, he will create the fear in you that if he is not there, you will not be able to manage things. You will start believing that if he is not there, your smooth activities will be disturbed, whether it is your company or your house or any other place.

He creates the deep idea in you that he is an important part in your life and without him you cannot run. He creates the fear in you. Then, depending on the level and the intensity of fear, he starts exploiting you.

In the same way, the first thing the ego does is to try to clearly prove to your being that you cannot live in your body and mind without it. It creates the fear that you cannot live without personality. Once you are frightened, once you are afraid, once you start believing that you cannot live in your body and mind without the ego, it is very easy for your ego to exploit you, to cheat you. Be very clear, it is just simple fear, nothing but simple fear.

For the blind man, the walking stick was just an extra accessory which he will realize he does not need once he gets his eyesight. In the same way, you carry your identity as an accessory because of the association with the ego.

Ahankara and Mamakara - Outer world identity and Inner world identity

We all have two identities, the identity that we project to the outer world, and the identity that we believe to be us in the inner world.

The identity which you believe to be you inside your mind is called *mamakar* in Sanskrit. It will always be much smaller than what you really are.

You will be carrying or remembering all your failures, past mistakes and guilt and constantly trying to work on them.

The identity which you project to the outer world is called *ahankar*.

Ahankar is your visiting card. You print everything that you want others to know about yourself. This is based on the identity you show to the outer world. It will always be more than what you have, what you are. It will always be much more than what you are because you think you have to sell yourself. It becomes a basic need especially in the societies where you have to market yourself.

Ahankar will be based on a superiority complex. Mamakar will be based on an inferiority complex. Ahankar will be based on fear, mamakar will be based on greed.

At this point, you don't trust that you can run your life without fear or greed, without the identity that you are carrying. The identity that you show to the outer world will always be based on fear. This is why it will be always more than what is. You will constantly be trying to keep it alive.

The identity that you carry in the inner world is based on greed. This is why you are always trying to develop the identity that you are carrying inside you. You will constantly be working on the identity that you believe is you and you will continue to try to chisel it.

You remember your past mistakes in your mind so that you will not repeat them. You want to update yourself; as such, you will remember only those things. You will not remember your big achievements; only others will remember your achievements. You mostly remember only your mistakes and failures.

When you measure yourself in the inner world, inside your mind, you measure yourself based upon the weakest link of the chain. When you project to the outer world, you project yourself based on the strongest link of the chain.

Your life is nothing but the fight between these two worlds.

The conflict between *ahankar* and *mamakar*, the conflict between the personality that you show to the outer world and the personality that you reveal in your inner world is called 'tension'.

The uneasy feeling between these two identities creates dis-easeness. The dis-easeness between these two identities is the disease. Understand this basic thing.

Both the identities *ahankar* and *mamakar* are pure myths; both are lies. You are something beyond these two identities.

You constantly spend your life trying to protect these two identities. When they start growing, they start fighting with each other and start giving you trouble. It is like marrying two women at a time and having both of them living with you at the same time! These two identities are not only lies; they do not exist in you either. You are something far more than these two identities that you are carrying around in your life.

If you are spending your whole energy expanding *ahankar*, the identity that you project to the outer world, your life becomes materialistic. If you are spending your whole life chiseling and developing *mamakar*, the identity that you think is you, your whole life becomes moralistic and suppressing.

Working on *ahankar* leads to a materialistic life. People who work on *mamakar* are constantly working on their personality, constantly working on creating some identity to feel satisfied. Working in the outer world with *ahankar* and working in the inner world with *mamakar*, both lead to more and more suffering, difficulties or depression.

The basic truth is that you are much more than these two identities. When you un-clutch from these two identities, you will suddenly realize that you are beyond the two identities. At this point, these two can never bind you again.

Now, I will spend few minutes answering your questions, because I have expressed too many new concepts. Unless you question, you will not be able to digest what I have said.

One more thing. Usually you feel, 'If I ask questions, everyone will look at me and I may look like a fool.' Please understand, if you ask your question, you may look like a fool. However, if you do not ask, you will *be* a fool! It is better to look like a fool and have an answer than to be a fool without the answer.

One more thing, unless you analyze these concepts with questions and answers, you will not be able to internalize this truth. You will not be able to make this an experience in you.

Questions and Answers

Q: You were telling us about enlightenment. Can you explain the process of your enlightenment?

A: Nice question, but too early to ask. Do you want an honest answer or do you want a socially polite answer?

(Questioner says, 'Honest answer'.)

You will have to wait until the third day for an honest answer. If I were to speak about my enlightenment at this point, you would not be able to connect to it. You would not be able to accept it. You see, unless you have one glimpse of meditation or truth from me, you will not be able to trust my experience.

Unless you experience the technology that I have created, you will not be able to relate to it. If I start speaking about my enlightenment, you will either start believing it out of politeness or questioning it. Neither of these will be helpful to you at this point. Neither will arguing help nor will believing help. You may even just take it as one more story. Even that will not help you. It may look like one more fiction story or an interesting novel but that is not going to help you. Just have a little patience.

Over the next two days, you will have at least one glimpse of clarity, peace, rest or at least one moment of deep relaxation. Once that happens in you, you will be able to trust. You

might then think, 'Oh! If this can happen to me, it could have happened to him also.' Unless you get that glimpse, you will not be able to trust that the other person has had the experience. So I request you to please wait. I will surely speak about my personal experience.

Unless you yourself get a glimpse, you will not be able to relate with what I am saying. Even if I were to tell you, it would just be one more story. It will not be an inspiration for you. I will keep it as a last weapon to inspire you! My enlightenment story should inspire you and make you work towards that experience. If I speak about my experience when you are truly ready to hear about it, it will be an inspiration for you to work towards that same state. It can be an inspiration to make you express or grow towards the same state. So please wait.

Q: This question is about the point that you mentioned about happiness. I was explaining to my son that I am happy as a result of my learnings from these discourses. He replied, 'I am already happy. Why do you want me to do anything else?'

A: We relate ourselves with things that we think is happiness. If he is really happy already, let him be happy. Don't bother; let him be happy.

Q: That is what I thought, but at the same time I could not explain to him what kind of happiness I am experiencing. I think for a person to proceed he must know what real happiness is.

A: You have to understand two things.

First, if someone feels that something is giving them happiness, let them be. Only life can teach them, you cannot teach them. All of you be very clear, you cannot teach anyone, only life can teach.

Second, unless they need help, you cannot help them. If you try to help without them seeking your help, it will be like the boy scout story. What happened to the boy scouts? You will be doing the same thing that they were doing. When they need your help let them come. Otherwise, only life can teach them. Your idea of happiness and unhappiness has come out of your experience. Please be honest and clear, did you listen to your father when you were young? No! You did not.

Q: Actually we did listen to our fathers. This generation is different.

A: To tell you honestly, I am not able to believe this statement. No son listens to his father. People forget that they did not listen to their fathers only after they become fathers and have a vested interest in that position. They remember only the incidents that they listened to their fathers because they have to train their sons. They do not remember the incidents where they said 'no' to their fathers.

I tell you one simple, basic thing. You feel that you are a man only when you say 'no' to your father. Until then you feel that you are a child. You start saying 'no' to your father just to prove that you are a man. It is the basic psychology. When you say 'no' you think that you are somebody. So please be very clear, whatever you say, your son is going to say 'no', because he wants to be somebody.

I read a beautiful passage in a book. One man says, 'I found three ways to get things done.' His friend asks, 'What are the three ways?'

The man replies, 'First, do it by yourself. Second, hire someone to do it. Third, tell your kids not to do it! That's all, it will be done. Tell your kids not to do something and it will definitely be done.'

Whenever you say anything, your child is just waiting to say 'no' to it. Saying 'no' to you creates a deep courage and strength in him. It makes him feel that he is a man; now he is on his own. We need to understand that we also said 'no' to our elders. Later on in the old age because you started having the

problem of selective amnesia or because you started remembering only the incidents in which you said 'yes', you forget thousands of incidents in which you said 'no' to your elders. Be very clear, your kids are doing the same thing that you did.

Only life can teach them. You can neither teach nor help your children unless they want help. If you force something on them, if you force rules and regulations on them, they may learn one thing, how to cheat you, that's all. If you start forcing, they will listen to the same words without respect.

Let us face the reality; let us come to a practical situation. I am not ready to give any idealistic solution. Please understand: I don't want to give any big theories. I can give some ideas, like 'Take him to some temple,' 'Take him to some God,' 'Take him to some guru.' But nothing will come out of it. I tell you, nothing will happen.

And especially these days, children have become so intelligent. See, the inner software is getting updated, which means intelligence is getting updated. Nothing can be done about it. When you were growing up, the emphasis was specialization; so elders were intelligent because they were experienced in specialization of some sort, like their family business for example. So the son depended on the father for that knowledge in order to continue the business. But these days, the emphasis is on updating knowledge; so the younger generation is more updated and intelligent than your generation!

Be very clear, in the past, lifestyle emphasized and valued specialization. Naturally elders were more intelligent. Today, it is more important to be able to access information and update your knowledge. Naturally youngsters will be intelligent. All you need is to drop your ego and respect youngsters. That is the only thing that can be done. Nothing else can be done because fortunately or unfortunately the whole social setup has turned from specialization to updating. So be ready to respect the next generation.

Q: When you were talking about the concept, you said we are not the body, we are not the mind, we are not the ego. But in the process, what are we? You also talked about dropping the ego and then about our functioning independent of the ego. But if the 'I' itself is not the element of the ego and even if we drop the ego and we say, 'Now I am not the ego but I am functioning,' is that also not an aspect of the ego itself? Then who am I? Am I just the thought? Am I the consciousness or what am I?

A: Beautiful questions. But I really suspect if you really need answers! Please understand, people who need answers will put only one question. A person who puts several questions continuously needs only experience. He cannot be given answers.

First, you assumed so many things and you say, 'If I drop the ego and start saying that I am living without ego, is it not ego?' The moment you drop the ego you will not say I am living without ego.

Somebody asked a Zen master, 'Master, how will I come to know whether I am enlightened or not?' The master says, 'If you are enlightened, this very doubt will disappear. As long as you have the doubt whether you are enlightened or not, you are not enlightened.'

He says beautifully that the moment a person becomes enlightened, the doubt *'Am I enlightened or not?'* will disappear. In the same way, the thought, *'I am enlightened'* will also disappear. He will neither have the doubt whether he is enlightened or not nor will he have the ego that he is enlightened. Both will not be there.

So in the hypothetical question, 'If I drop my ego and I start saying I am living without ego, is it not one more ego?' the very hypothesis is wrong. If you drop your ego,

you will not say you are living without ego – that is the first thing.

Next thing, you are asking, 'If I am not body, mind or ego, then who am I?'

You need to ask that to yourself, not to me. I asked and I found the answer. I am asking you to ask yourself. I am not here to answer your questions. I am here to question your answers. You have so many answers to the question, 'Who am I?' You have the answer, 'I am the body, I am the mind, I am the ego.' So I am questioning all your answers. No, you are not body, you are not the mind, and you are not the ego.

I will leave you alone with your question. When I leave you alone with your question, your question will become a quest. And that quest will naturally make you experience the truth.

Please do not ask these questions to me. Ask these questions to yourself. I am not actually answering your question. I am questioning your answers. So this question, 'Who am I?' should not be asked to me; it should be asked to you.

Q: You explained everything very beautifully today. Are tomorrow and day after tomorrow's classes really necessary?

A: That's nice. I tell you one thing: if you have truly understood, you do not need the classes given over the next two days. If you have not understood, again you do not need the classes. If you feel that you are almost catching the essence of these concepts, and that you think you should listen a little more, then you need tomorrow's and day after tomorrow's classes.

So be very clear, if you have really understood, you don't need the next two discourses. And I tell you, if you really understood, not just tomorrow or day after tomorrow, you cannot forget me at any time! You will simply start living with me. I am not talking about the physical level; I am talking about the conscious level. If you understood this one session, what I talked about in this one class, not only do you not need the later classes, you will start radiating these teachings in your whole life. So if you have understood clearly, you don't need anymore. And if you have not understood completely, again you don't need more. If you feel, 'I understood a few things; I think I need some more,' then you are welcome tomorrow.

Q: You have been talking about purposelessness; life must be purposeless. Having been born in this world, we have to grow, we have to have some commitments and when the time comes we have to end our lives also. Given this situation, there is a feeling that we have to cultivate that which is purposelessness. But then we have some commitments in life, we have some goals in our practical day-to-day lives. How are we to balance this? How do we understand this?

A: First thing, I am not asking you to cultivate the feeling of purposelessness, because it is the pure truth. You don't need to cultivate it; it is the simple truth. You should understand the purposelessness. The attitude of purposelessness need not be cultivated in you. It is a simple truth; all you need to do is understand it.

Whether you believe it or not, your life is not under your control, am I right? Whether you believe it or not, you will not know when the end will come, am I right? Are you sure you will reach your house safely today? I am not sure. I don't know about you, but I am not sure whether I will reach the ashram safely in this Bangalore traffic!

Whether you understand it or not, accept it or not, believe it or not - this is the truth. I am opening the truth, which is the ultimate truth. Let the truth take its own course. Why should you be so afraid? Why are you afraid to enter into the truth, to let the truth penetrate you? Let it work. Before entering into the truth itself you are afraid – 'I have a

family to support, I have professional responsibilities, I have social commitments. If I enter into the truth, what will happen to my life?'

The small wave is afraid, what will happen to it if it drops into the ocean, what will happen to the pebbles which it collected. When the wave is rising, it tells the next wave, 'You are my wife, please stand here; you are my daughter, please stand there... I have a commitment towards all of you. I have to do this, I have to do that.' And suddenly the wave disappears. Not only that wave, but all the other waves also disappear into the ocean!

What I am saying is the truth. If you can enter into the truth with courage, you will be a much better husband, a much better father and a much better family person. But only after entering into it, each one of you will be able to understand. Now the question that you are asking is a hypothetical question just like how the blind person asks, 'I understand that I will get my eyesight; but how will I walk without my stick?' I tell you, if you understand the beauty of purposelessness without this fear, you will be able to fulfill your commitments more beautifully.

*Enlightenment –
         Guaranteed!!*

न त्वं विप्रादिको वर्णो नाश्रमी नाक्षगोचरः ।
असङ्गोऽसि निराकारो विश्वसाक्षी सुखी भव ॥

धर्माधर्मौ सुखं दुःखं मानसानि न ते विभो ।
न कर्तासि न भोक्तासि मुक्त एवासि सर्वदा ॥

Chapter 2

You do not belong to Brahmana
or any other caste or to any ashrama,
You are not visible to the eyes.
Unattached, formless and witness of all are you, be blissful.

Virtue and vice, pleasure and pain are of the mind, not of you.
Oh all-pervading, you are neither doer, nor enjoyer.
Verily you are ever free.

Today's subject is Enlightenment – Guaranteed!! In the previous chapter we saw, Enlightenment - It Is Possible!

The first thing that we need to understand is that enlightenment is possible. From time immemorial, there has been a conflict or fight among our sages. One group of sages says there is something called enlightenment. The other group says there is no such thing as enlightenment.

Fact vs Truth

The people who say that there is something called enlightenment state the fact. People who say that there is no such thing as enlightenment state the truth. The first group gives the fact that there is something called enlightenment. The second group by saying there is

no enlightenment, creates a technique for enlightenment.

The concept that there is no enlightenment is a technique to make us enlightened. Just by having the idea that there is enlightenment, we tend to make enlightenment our goal. The moment we make it our goal we miss the goal. Anybody who makes enlightenment a goal always misses it. Enlightenment is not the goal. It is the very path itself.

Please understand, if we are not able to realize the truth when the Master speaks, if we do not feel the effect of his words the very moment the air that comes from him reaches our ears, we can forget about the words. When we carry this as a memory in our mind, we will always give it our own meaning.

When we start giving our meaning from the memory of the words we carry, we will create double trouble: first we will torture ourselves, and next, we will vomit these words on others and torture them.

I often tell my audience when I speak in Tamil (language spoken in southern India) that people who do not understand Tamil are lucky; they do not understand the meaning of the words I speak. Those who think they understand what I say actually do not understand. Their dictionary is different from mine and they distort my words. They misunderstand and misinterpret me with the filtered product of their minds. In the process of doing so, they lose the truth. Those who do not understand the words at least focus on the energy and are benefited.

From time immemorial in the *vedic* system of India, the spiritual nerve center of the world, there have been two kinds of *rishis* or seers. One group continuously says that there is enlightenment; these are the descendants of Sankara. The other group says that there is no such thing as enlightenment; they are the descendants of Buddha. The former says *poorna* - complete; the latter group says *shoonya* - void. But both of them are leading to the same reality.

One group states the fact and the other group states the truth. We need to understand these two words, fact and truth. Fact is the idea stated as it is, plainly as we understand it. Truth is the word that we may not understand with our mind, but the moment we work with that word, suddenly something opens up in our being and we end up in the truth.

All the Hindu *purana*, the epics, are based on the truth and cannot be tested for factual accuracy. When Valmiki (author of the great epic Ramayana) talks about the population of monkeys in Kishkindha, it is factually impossible that so many monkeys lived in such a small place. Valmiki is talking about the truthful energy of the monkeys, not the factual number.

When Sankara says that there is enlightenment, *poorna*, he inspires you to work towards it. He creates tremendous inspiration. When the tremendous inspiration is created, automatically all other goals, all other ideas are dropped from your mind. The moment Buddha says it is *shoonya*, there is no such thing as enlightenment or *poorna*, there is no need for you to run, there is no need for you to search. Immediately, the tremendous energy which is created in you, in the name of search, starts falling into itself. It is directed towards itself. The moment the energy is directed towards itself, it becomes enlightenment!

Desire without object is enlightenment.

When you have some strong desire with object, you work towards that object. But if the object is removed and the same strong pull, desire and energy turns towards itself, you will realize yourself. When Masters say that there is nothing called enlightenment, they are breaking our goal-oriented mind and they are bringing us to this present moment.

Ramana Maharshi talks of this practice in India:

In the Indian villages they burn the dead bodies in the graveyard. When they burn the dead bodies, they use a stick. They use a bamboo stick to burn dead bodies so that the body doesn't fall over to one side or the other. When the body is completely burnt they throw the stick also into the same fire and burn it.

In the same way when Sankara says there is enlightenment, he uses that word as a stick. With that stick he burns all other desires in you. Automatically the idea of enlightenment attracts you so much that all other desires are burnt. Finally this last desire, enlightenment, is also dropped in the same fire and it disappears. Then you are enlightened!

On the other side, when Buddha says there is no enlightenment he simply creates a space. He creates an inner void in which you can directly drop. Millions and millions of saints and *rishis* have come to this planet Earth. They can be categorized into these two groups, one group that says there is enlightenment and the other group that says there is no enlightenment.

Whether you believe it or not, masters from both the groups are leading to the same goal. I can give hundreds and hundreds of examples in the tradition of Sankara, including Madhva and Ramanuja. You may ask, 'Madhva and Ramanuja are different. How can they all be in Sankara's category?' Whoever says there is the ultimate stage, whoever fixes the goal, all of them come under the category of Sankara including Madhva, Ramanuja, Ramakrishna, Chaitanya and Meera. All these masters talk about *poorna*. They are all in the tradition of Sankara.

In the other group, we can again give many examples: Buddha, Nagarjuna, Bodhidharma and all the Zen masters. Some masters state the fact while some masters state the truth. But both are leading us to the ultimate, which simply is enlightenment. I can say that because the word 'enlightenment' is loaded with too much meaning, the word is completely corrupted. Because of this, some masters have to say that this word cannot be used.

Whether we use that word or we do not use that word, the experience that we achieve in the end, the *poorna* or the ultimate bliss, does exist. It is possible to be in the state where we feel we are no longer bound by the body and mind; that stage does exist.

Enlightenment Guaranteed

Whether we speak in the language of Sankara or in the language of Buddha, there is something which is beyond our body and mind. That is what I wanted to emphasize by the name of the discourse, 'Enlightenment - It Is Possible!!'

I am not giving you any false guarantees. Be very clear that I am speaking the truth. See, in the outer world, the big problem is, whenever you give something away, whatever you have will be reduced by the very act of giving away. It is not that people don't want to give. They want to give but they want to have for themselves as well.

The conflict between having and giving is the whole problem. That is why we cannot even criticize the people who go around making promises and guarantees which they don't intend to fulfill because each one has their own understanding. We cannot criticize any individual being; each one has his or her own idea.

See, if they give something that they have, they will have lesser than when they started. But let me be very clear: what I have will never be reduced even if I give it to another. This is the reason that I can continuously give. I cannot take pride that I continue to give because what I give is never diminished. When I share it, it only grows. It is the quality of the object that is being given, not the quality of me.

Let me be honest, it is because of the nature of what I am giving that I am constantly sharing. By sharing, it only grows. If I too had the same objects of the outer world, which would reduce when given to others, I don't know whether I would give them away or not!

If you were to come and ask me for this *rudraksha mala* (rosary made out of beads from rudraksha tree) that I am wearing, I don't know whether I will give it or not. But I can say one thing, what I am giving always grows. By sharing, it only expands, it only grows.

If you can realize these words, if you can understand these words that I am speaking, you may also have the same property - the one that expands by giving. You can have the wisdom or knowledge which will grow by sharing.

Understand the Truth This Very Moment

All that I request from you is to try and understand this concept this very moment. If you miss it, do not worry. However, do not carry the corpse; do not carry the dead words home. Try to forget everything after going home. I always create a lot of contradicting statements so that you will stop thinking about them. Either you understand now when the words are stated or you will never understand by carrying just the words home with you. You will only create one more philosophy.

When Sankara said that there is enlightenment, if the disciples had understood at that point, there would have been no need to create any books. Half of his disciples who did not understand took some notes and created books. Taking notes and creating books caused confusion. The whole problem is taking notes and creating books. When you take notes you can catch only the verbal language; you don't catch the body language.

Be very clear, verbal language is not going to help. Only body language is going to help. When I speak these words, it is the confidence radiated in my eyes, the honesty radiated in my body language that is going to work on you, not the words that I am speaking. If you want just the words that I am stating, there are hundreds of books written.

Once I went to the bookstore, Landmark. I did not publish a single book for the next three months. I felt that there is so much literature. When there are so many books already, what is the need for me to add more confusion!

When the disciples start taking notes and publishing books, the confusion starts. Then enlightenment becomes philosophy; it becomes a theory and it becomes a goal. People start working towards it and start creating more and more conflicts. Once that one conflict or one problem is created, immediately all the other problems are created.

Just Listen; You Will Express

Ashtavakra's words are so powerful that they are pure technology. There is no need for you to work on these words. These words are so powerful that they will simply work on you. Also, the words are so powerful that just listening to them can make the ultimate happen in you.

In *Vedanta* there are three steps: *sravana, manana* and *nidhidhyasana* - listening, contemplating and expressing the truth in your life. *Sravana* means listening, *manana* means contemplating, *nidhidhyasana* means expressing.

With Ashtavakra's concepts, you have only two steps. Just listen; you will automatically express! No *manana*, just *sravana* and then straightaway to *nidhidhyasana*. It is not possible for you to do *manana* with your mind given that it is completely polluted and corrupted. Any *manana* done with this mind will only create more and more trouble.

The Fearful Mind Escapes through Hypothetical Questions

The mind is filled with fears, worries and sorrows. That is why when one person asked me, 'If I drop the mind and I become enlightened, and I say I am working without mind, will it not become one more ego?' This question is just like asking, 'If my son gets married and then his mother–in-law comes and calls me, how will she address me? And what will the mother-in-law's daughter-in-law or daughter-in-law's mother-in-law be calling me? How should the relationship be? How should I talk to them?'

First have the son, then let him get married, then let the mother-in-law come and then you will see, naturally some sort of relationship will develop. Before anything happens, when you imagine too much and create too many hypothetical questions before anything has happened, it is because of your fear of entering into the experience.

When you are afraid to enter into the reality, when you are frightened to face the truth, you create hypothetical questions. Hypothetical questions are shields that you use to protect yourself from the truth. The mind which creates hypothetical questions is deeply centered on fear. When you are centered on fear, not only do you create problems for yourself, you create problems for others also.

A small story:

> A newly married couple went to a hotel. For some reason the wife was afraid that the hotel room was bugged. She ordered the husband to check the room. You know how these newly married men serve their wives! The man started checking behind the curtain, near the window, under the carpet, under the bed sheet, under the bed, etc. Finally under the bed, he found a mysterious plate bolted. With all his power he removed the nut, took

the bolt out, threw the plate away and then they felt very relaxed.

The next day morning the hotel manager asked, 'Sir, how are you? How is your room? Is everything ok?'

The guy asked, 'Why are you asking me so many questions?'

The manager said, 'Sir, we don't know how it happened. The people who stayed in the room below you were complaining that the chandelier fell on them!'

When you are centered on fear, you create problems for yourself and create problems for others. Be very clear, anything done based on fear will only create more and more problems. When you are centered on fear, you are constantly creating hypothetical questions to shield yourself from the truth, from reality.

You are not more powerful than reality; you are not more powerful than the truth. Reality or truth forcefully takes the shield out of your hands. That is what you refer to as 'depression' or 'feeling lonely'. Whatever you use as a shield, whatever you use to protect yourself from the truth, the truth will take it away from you.

Vivekananda says beautifully, 'Renounce gracefully, otherwise it will be snatched from you. Relax gracefully, otherwise you will be made to rest. Either you go to the church or six people will carry you there. Don't wait until six people carry you there.' Understand, either you do it gracefully or simply the truth will make it happen for you.

Parashakti, Existence, the truth, is so powerful that you cannot work against it. You cannot do anything against reality. It is like some fish swim along with the current, while some fish always like to go against the current. There are some people who have only one word in their mind, 'No.' Anything you say, their response would be, 'No.' It is like when people get married, they start as *'sona'* - gold.

Just after a few years, just one 'I' will enter, *'suniye'* - listen. First it will start with *sona* and then it will end up in *suniye*! When you have this attitude, constantly you will say, 'No', 'No', 'No'. It will be the standard response.

Saying 'No' - The Way of the Ego

The mind that constantly says 'no' can never grasp anything. It can never see reality. You yourself don't actually know why you are constantly saying 'no'. Actually you feel that you are great when you say 'no' or when you criticize someone. It gives you a sense of importance.

Let me tell you a small story:

> There was a young man living in a village. His problem was that the whole village knew that he was a fool and as a result no one respected him. Everyone called him a fool and *buddhu* - dumb. Even the children called him *buddhu*. He wanted a solution to his problem.
>
> He heard that an enlightened master was coming to his village. He went to the master and said, 'Master, please teach me something; give me some technique or some method so that people think of me as an intelligent person.'
>
> He did not ask to become intelligent. If he had asked that he should become intelligent, the master would have given the right technique. But his request was that people should think of him as an intelligent person.
>
> The master said, 'Alright! I will give you one technique. Practice the technique for one week. Within a week the whole village will think that you are the most intelligent person. Be very clear that you will not become intelligent but the

whole village will say that you are intelligent.'

He said, 'Ok, that is what I wanted. I do not care about anything else. I am not asking that I should become intelligent. Just make sure that the whole village considers me to be an intelligent person.'

The master said, 'You need to do only one thing. Your response to anything should be to simply disagree and criticize. If somebody says this moon is beautiful, tell them, 'Ha, what is there? Where is the beauty? Prove to me where the beauty is.' If somebody says this rose is beautiful, ask them, 'Where is the beauty? A rose is a rose; where is the beauty in it?' If somebody says it is ugly, ask them, 'What? It is so beautiful; where is the ugliness?' Simply, disagree and criticize; whatever people say, criticize. Nothing else needs to be done.'

After one week the master came back to the village. The moment he entered the village he saw this man under a big neem tree sitting on the throne on the stage. All the elders were sitting down and listening to him. He had practically become a guru.

The master went up to him and asked, 'How are you?'

This guy who had now become a guru asked, 'Who are you?'

The master said, 'I am the *swami* who came one week ago.'

The guy said, 'Oh, is it so? Now I am busy with the class. Meet me after the class. Please wait.'

The man had become so popular and the whole village had started respecting him. It is a simple technique; just start criticizing anything and everything.

The whole crowd will start respecting you as an intelligent being.

Please be very clear about the mind that says 'no.' People may respect you as an intelligent person. But inside, not only will you have a void but constantly yjou will also have confusion because you are trying to protect yourself from the truth.

The moment you start saying 'yes,' the truth will come inside you and work on you and teach you. That is why I always tell people, 'Even though you may be exploited, try to say 'yes.'

You may say, 'Master, what is this? You are asking us to be fools.' I am not asking you to be fools. Be very clear, sometimes you are protecting yourself too much. Whenever you think that others are exploiting you, it is simply the result of your efforts to exploit them. When they don't allow you to exploit them, you say that they are exploiting you.

See, all the countries claim that their army is a defensive army. Then who is the offensive army? Similarly everybody claims their anger is just to defend themselves. Then who is really offending them?

Be very clear, that is the reason I tell you, either your mind will cheat you by allowing you to think that you are being exploited or someone else may cheat you by really exploiting you. Someone else may cheat you only once in a while; but your mind will cheat you all the time, all 24 hours in the day. If someone else cheats you a few times, you can count them, they are just a few in number. But if you let your mind cheat you, you are cheated for your whole life. It will swallow your whole life. Your whole life will be swallowed by your mind.

The attitude of saying 'no' will not let you protect yourself. It will constantly torture you inside. The weapon that you create to protect yourself will start killing you. Like the electric fence that you create to protect yourself may kill even you, it could kill you. You create this weapon of saying 'no' just to protect yourself. But it just kills you.

Listen with a complete, open attitude. Ashtavakra's words are so powerful they can work on you right away. It can do the miracle which Sankara calls enlightenment, what Buddha calls nirvana.

Why So Many Enlightened Masters from India

When I travel to other countries many people ask me, 'Why are there so many enlightened masters in India? Why are there so many *swamis* in India? Why are there so many spiritual gurus in India? Why aren't there as many from other countries?'

I always tell people, 'Premature babies, like the ones born in the seventh or eighth month, need incubators which supply oxygen and all the other needs, to take care of the babies. Please understand, I am not saying immature babies. We are all immature babies! I am talking about premature babies. Premature babies need incubators to take care of them. In the same way, India is a spiritual incubator for enlightened masters to land.'

It is true that only India has produced so many spiritual masters who travel all over the world. India represents spirituality in the whole world. India is highly respected only in this field. India always has legitimate competition in other fields. In this field, India has no competitors, it is the clear leader. India is the *jagadguru*, guru for the whole world continuously producing enlightened masters. As long as India continues to produce enlightened masters, this culture cannot be shaken.

You may say there are many problems in India. You may say, 'Master, there are political problems, social problems and economic problems.' See, each country supplies or contributes something to planet Earth. Unless

the whole humanity feels the need for that country, that country cannot exist. As far as India is concerned, humanity needs India just for enlightened masters.

Whether you want it or not, whether you accept it or not, spiritual talks will always be reaching your ears. If I am not here, tomorrow some other *swami* will be sitting here and speaking. Day after tomorrow some other *swami* will sit and speak.

Let me tell you, by abusing one *swami* or by disturbing one master, India's spirituality can never be destroyed. People think that by disrespecting one spiritual person or by disrespecting one spiritual master, India's spirituality can be disturbed. No. If I am not here, tomorrow some other Ananda will sit on the throne and speak the same words.

Spirituality - The Backbone of India

Spirituality has become the backbone, lifeblood of the Indian system. Whether you want it or not, words like enlightenment, meditation and temple will constantly come to your ears. You cannot do anything about it. When these words are continuously heard by your ears, you will naturally start thinking about them; you will start analyzing them.

Whatever you see or hear continuously will start working on you. In India when you travel on the highway you will see many temples. If you live in any Indian village, you will be constantly hearing these words - *Ramayana*, *Mahabharata*, meditation or something else which will inspire you and direct you to the Ultimate.

Be very clear, so many of you are sitting here and listening to *Ashtavakra Gita*, because you all have heard enough of *Ramayana*,

Mahabharata, purana and all these concepts. You have already heard enough of basic level concepts and now you can start working on yourself straight away. In India whether you want it or not, whether you understand it or not, whether you accept it or not, these ideas are constantly sent inside. They are presented to you in one way or another.

The cream of India's intelligence promotes spirituality. In most of the other countries, the best and brightest spend their energy doing business. In India the cream of the country, the intelligent people, spend their energy spreading the spiritual truth.

Amongst the hundred million people of India, there are thirteen million *swamis*. In a village in India, two million people will gather for spiritual functions. You do not have to go to a city to have this experience; one village is enough. For Kumbha Mela, the sacred Hindu pilgrimage, seventy million people gather. India truly is a spiritual incubator.

You are Beyond Societal Conditionings

Let us enter into the *Ashtavakra Gita*.

The fourth *sutra*:

> *You do not belong to Brahmana or any other caste or to any ashrama,*
> *You are not visible to the eyes.*
> *Unattached, formless and witness of all are you, be blissful.*
> *Virtue and vice, pleasure and pain are of the mind, not of you.*
> *Oh all-pervading, you are neither doer, nor enjoyer.*
> *Verily you are ever free.*

Yesterday, one of my devotees asked me, 'Master, I have seen you speaking for the last two years. This is the first time that I see you using a book when you are speaking.' To tell you honestly, I am only speaking about two or three *sutras* everyday. I could simply repeat the *sutra* directly.

I read from the book because the words in these *sutras* are so similar to my own words. If asked to write a *sutra*, I would write these same words. People should not think I have written these *sutras*. These *sutras* are written by Ashtavakra. I bring the book so that people understand that they are not written by me. Ashtavakra is using the very words, 'Be blissful'.

Ashtavakra says to Janaka, '*You are not a Brahmana.*' You need to understand this important statement.

You do not belong to the Brahmana or any other caste or to any ashrama.

You are not visible to the eyes. Unattached, formless and witness of all are you, be happy.

Ashtavakra wants to tell Janaka that he does not belong to any community, any *dharma* or any *ashrama*. He does not belong to any *varnashrama-dharma*. *Varna* means the four categories of social divisions: *brahmana,* *vaishya, kshatriya* and *shudra*. *Ashrama* means the four different stages in life: *brahmacharya, grihastha, vanaprastha* and *sannyasa*. There are four categories in *varna* and *ashrama* each.

Ashtavakra tells Janaka that he does not belong to any of these four categories. One more thing: *vedic* seers are the only courageous people to say that the system which they themselves have created is not sufficient. *vedic rishis* are the most modern-minded people.

Knowledge is Free and Open to Updating

With the internet, most knowledge and information is free. Anybody can access information, comment on that information, discuss the information with other interested parties, and ultimately update the information. Successful CEOs share the philosophy that knowledge is free and disseminate it freely within their organizations and with their customers. This is not to say that patents and trademarks have disappeared; but, the most visionary of executives recognize that it is in everyone's best interest for them to publicly share their knowledge and allow people to improve upon it or update it. As a result, everyone will end up with a better product and their companies will flourish.

Our *rishis* had both these qualities.

In India firstly, knowledge is and has always been free; whether you receive it or not is up to you. The masters are constantly speaking about the truth. Teachings on spirituality are continuously given. Knowledge is free.

Secondly, Indian *rishis* are so courageous that they keep the whole thing open. They say we can update their work; we are free to interpret their work.

Here Ashtavakra is declaring that the *vedic* system is not the truth. He is declaring very clearly that the community system has also been created by the *rishis*. He is very courageous to say that we are beyond that. The community system was created for practical reasons; and it is used only for certain purposes. It is not life itself. Being a doctor is only your profession; *you* are not a doctor. Do not identify yourself with your profession.

Indian masters are constantly abused and disrespected on the international stage, because India's poverty is projected all the time. And why should the media project poverty? There is no need to do so. There is no need, India has enough. All that the Indian people need to do is share amongst themselves. India has enough; just sharing is necessary, nothing else is needed.

Because of this image projected by some of the media to the whole world, I am always questioned, 'Master, you speak about so many things, it is nice. But why have the Indians created the caste system? Why have they created so many superstitions?'

Be very clear about two things, I am not justifying the caste system. But let me explain why it was created and how our masters expected us to use that system. We have in fact, abused the system. We cannot blame the person who created the knife just because we do not know how to use a knife. We cannot blame the person who invented electricity just because we got an electric shock.

Please be very clear why the system was created and how we have abused it. The system was created basically to make us grow, to help us grow from step one to step two, from step two to step three and so on.

One important thing you should understand: human beings are social animals. They cannot live alone. They have to live together with other humans. When we live as a group, naturally we will create a social system; we will create a group. At least in India, the community system was created based on knowledge and intelligence. In many other countries, their community system is based on money and power.

The Vedic Community System Based on Knowledge and Attitude, Not on Birth

Ashtavakra is a great *rishi*. He is not speaking today; he spoke ten thousand years ago. This book was written at least five thousand years before the *Bhagavad Gita* which itself is at least five thousand years old. So ten thousand years ago, he is boldly declaring, 'You are not *Brahmana* and you don't belong to any other community. You are beyond all those things.'

Note one interesting thing, when Ashtavakra addresses Janaka he should have said, 'You are not *Kshatriya*' - the warrior class, because Janaka is a king. But Ashtavakra says, 'You are not *Brahmana*,' the intellectual class. What does that mean? It means that in those days the community system was based on knowledge, and not on birth.

A master constantly observes how a person is showing his energy and interest towards knowledge. He also observes how he is working, his intensity and his attitude, and then decides whether that person is going to be a spiritual teacher or a merchant or a person who is going to rule the country or one who is going to be assisting the other three categories.

A person who has mostly time to share, belongs to worker class, *shudra*. A person who has intelligence and creates some products with his time and who shares these products is called *vaishya*; he belongs to the business class. A person who has confidence and shares his confidence with others and gives a sense of security is called *kshatriya*, the person who rules. A person who has knowledge, spiritual wisdom and who shares that with society is called *brahmana*.

Janaka was sharing his wisdom. He was more or less like a *yogi*. He was ruling the whole kingdom as a *yogi*, not as a king. That is why Ashtavakra says, 'You are not a *Brahmana*, nor do you belong to any other caste or any *ashrama*. You are *neither brahmana*, *kshatriya*, *vaishya* or the fourth category nor are you *brahmacharya*, *grihastha*, *vanaprastha* or *sannyas*. You do not belong to any of these four categories. You do not belong to the four *ashrama* or four *varna*. You are beyond all these things.

You are Not Visible to the Eyes

'You are not visible to the eyes.' This is an important idea that you need to understand.

Straightaway Ashtavakra says, *'You are not visible to the eyes.'*

If I tell you that you are not visible to the eyes, you will tell me to go and have an eye checkup.

A small story:

> A man enters a building and asks someone there, 'Doctor, do I need

glasses?' The person replies, 'You surely do, because this is a bank.'

Similarly, if I say that you are not visible, you will ask me to go and get my eyes checked. But Ashtavakra tells Janaka, *'You are not visible.'*

A great enlightened master, Nisargadatta Maharaj, lived in central India. One of his devotees asked him, 'Maharaj, you say enlightened people don't have *karma*. Then how is it that your body is functioning and how are you working?'

Maharaj says, 'I am not working, I am not functioning.'

The disciple asks, 'What is this? You are talking to me, what about that? You may not go to an office, you may not have any responsibilities, but you are talking to me, what about that?'

Maharaj says, 'I am not talking to you.' He continues, 'I am not talking to you.' It is very difficult to understand but it's the truth. He says, 'You feel as if I am talking because you see. It is because you see that you see me. It is because you wanted to hear me that you hear me, that's all.'

It is a very subtle concept.

Let me tell you about a small incident. Then it may be possible for you to understand what Ashtavakra says and what Nisargadatta Maharaj says.

One of our devotees is trying to write my biography. He has listened to me speaking about many small incidents from my life and has collected them. He has done a very nice job. In the last two and a half years from January 2003, almost three thousand DVDs and videos have been recorded. He patiently went through them and collected many incidents from my discourses. The biggest problem for him was that if he tried to write all the incidents that he collected chronologically, one should conclude that I should be at least sixty years old. But I am not even thirty yet!

He asked me, 'Master, how could so many things happen in hardly twenty-eight years? How can I even tell people so much has happened in such a short span of time? It is simply impossible.'

The Paramahamsa is untouched by the games of the fish

Then I told him a small story on how it has to be understood.

> There is a swan flying in the sky and its reflection falls on the lake below. When the reflection falls on the water, the fish in the lake start jumping with excitement. They think that a new fish has come. They go around it, admiring it intensely.
>
> Some fish start jumping on the swan, some fish start dancing around the swan and some fish start selling land around the swan. Some start making a fence saying this is the ashram for the swan. Some fish start claiming places around the swan saying they want to be around the swan. They do all this without knowing that it is only the reflection of the swan. They think that it is one more fish.
>
> Some fish start jumping on the reflection saying, 'Oh, this fish is so loving, so caring, so graceful and so beautiful.' Some fish start jumping on the other side and start saying, 'This fish is not taking care of me at all, this fish is not paying any attention to me. You all say it is caring and loving, but it is not caring and loving at all.'

Some fish have the idea that the reflection is very caring and loving and some fish have the idea it is not so loving and caring. Some fish make positive observations about the reflection and some fish make negative observations about the reflection.

The fish see the reflection moving by the very motion created by them in the water. After a while the fish even start fighting among themselves saying, 'I am closer to the swan than you are.'

Then slowly the swan moves to the other side, the American side. All the American fish gather and build one more ashram! Then the swan flies over the Canada side. All the Canadian fish get together and build one more ashram.

Suddenly the swan starts flying over ground. The reflection in the water disappears; it is not there. All the fish now start saying, 'Oh, the swan has disappeared, the swan is not here, what should we do?'

One important thing: some fish are praising, some fish are blaming, some fish are creating ashrams, some fish are playing around, some fish are going away, some fish are jumping, but the swan is not even aware of any of them; the swan doesn't even know about this activity! The swan is neither aware nor is it interested. If at all you are an intelligent fish, the moment you see the reflection, if you understand that this doesn't seem like a fish, then you will wonder, 'Where is it coming from?' If you then look up and see the swan, you can also start flying! You can also just start flying.

If you have started flying, you are intelligent. The purpose of the swan is achieved. If you are just fighting with other fish, playing with other fish, playing with the reflection, playing in the area where the reflection is happening, be very clear, you will be simply cheated, you will simply miss the whole thing. You will simply miss it.

From the swan's point of view, it neither knows that the fish are jumping nor does it know that they are fighting or they are praising. In the same way, Ashtavakra says, from the vision of the *atman* (soul), you are not visible. For the swan, you are not visible.

Be very clear, the fish are not visible to the swan. Only birds interested in the fish see them. Swans don't see the fish, because they don't have to eat them. Eagles have to eat the fish. This is why constantly they see the fish. Swans do not have to see them because there is no need for the swan to see them. The swan just flies.

Sometimes, fortunately or spontaneously the reflection falls on the lake. The few intelligent fish that get to see the reflection, try to look up and see the swan. The other foolish fish just jump around, dance around or fight around the reflection. Whether you fight, blame, praise, jump, dance or sing, the swan is not even aware of any of it.

Here Ashtavakra says, you are not visible because you are beyond everything. All you can do is one thing. The moment you see the reflection, the moment you are awed to see the Master and wonder how such a being can happen, that it is humanly impossible, then your intelligence should start working and ask, 'Where is it happening?'

Worship - a Cunning Escape from the Master's Teachings

Do not try to be physically around the Master. Do not start worshipping the Master. Worshipping is the worst form of crucifixion.

Romans avoided Jesus just by crucifying him. Hindus have avoided Krishna by worshipping him, that's all. People say, 'Krishna is great and whatever he says in the Bhagavad Gita is true, but we can't follow it. He is great, so he can communicate all these teachings, but we cannot follow them.' Be very clear: do not avoid the Masters by worshipping them.

When we start worshipping, the first thing we do is avoid the true object of worship. Sometimes when worshipping inspires us to follow them, worshipping is alright. However, if it creates a feeling of distance, be very clear, the first thing to do is to stop the worshipping.

If worshipping makes you feel deeply connected, then it is alright. If the worshipping does not make you feel connected or if it is not acting as an inspiration to follow the path or the teachings, be very clear, worshipping is not going to help.

Fortunately, we have not made statues of Ashtavakra and that is why the verses in the Ashtavakra Gita are so pure. If we had not started making statues of Krishna, we would have all started following the Bhagavad Gita. The moment we started to make statues, we have decided not to follow the Bhagavad Gita.

A person came to me and said, 'Master, I am too stressed and there is too much pain in my life. Give me some solution to overcome it.'

I gave him a Bhagavad Gita book. I had recently spoken on the eighteen volumes of Bhagavad Gita and I gave him a CD and DVD of the discourse also. I told him, 'Please listen to this. I have spoken on *Karma yoga* - the beauty of purposelessness. Please listen to this and understand. Then the inner healing will happen in you. The constant irritation that you carry will disappear.' One reason for the constant irritation that a person carries, is stress.

I told him, 'Listen to this CD and watch this Gita DVD.' Then he said, 'Master, I have a *Gita* book also in my house. I keep it in my *puja* room (prayer room) and worship it everyday.' I asked him, 'If you have a glass of milk in your house, would you drink it or keep it in the *puja* room and show *arati* (offering of prayer)?'

Gita is a glass of milk. Drink and enjoy it. Do not keep it in the *puja* room and start doing *arati*. Krishna is milk. It is based on this concept that Jesus says, 'Drink me.' You are supposed to drink Krishna, not worship him. If your worship inspires you to drink, then it is acceptable. But if the worshipping creates a distance, something is seriously wrong in your understanding.

Here Ashtavakra says, *you are not visible*.

The *sutra* says:

> *Unattached, formless and witness of all are you.*

You are unattached, you are formless and witness. You are beyond this body, you are beyond this mind. You are formless, unattached.

'Unattached' is a beautiful word. Ashtavakra says, '*You are unattached*'. I am also saying that you are unattached. Please do not just start believing it. Understand how you are unattached.

The Vicious Cycle of Guilt

One person came to me and said, 'Master, I constantly suffer because of my smoking habit. The moment I get up from bed, I cannot do anything else but smoke. I have to smoke, but after one hour I have a deep guilt. After two hours when I get ready to go to work, again I have to smoke; again an hour of guilt. What should I do? I am constantly suffering with this guilt, and I am always suffering with this habit. What should I do?'

I told him, 'Either you should drop smoking or drop the guilt. Drop any one thing; you will be liberated from this habit.'

He was shocked to hear that. He said, 'Master, you know that I am not able to stop smoking. If I drop the guilt, how do you say that I will drop smoking?'

I told him that it is a vicious circle. When you have guilt, what will you do? You will constantly keep repeating, 'I should drop smoking,' 'I should drop smoking.' Naturally what will happen? You will give power to the word 'smoking' in your mind. When you use the words, 'I should drop smoking,' you will remember the smoking. So the memory of smoking is again and again engraved in you deeper and deeper. The memory of smoking is engraved in your inner space deeper and deeper. How do you expect that you will be able to drop smoking?

Be Aware of the Words You Use Inside You

I always tell people, when they want to get rid of any disease, never repeat to themselves, 'I should get rid of this disease.' Instead create the words, 'I should become healthy.' Learn how to think, learn how to create the right words in you.

Please understand, the words that you create inside you are so powerful; straightaway they become reality.

The words which you repeat again and again in your life will become reality in your life.

If you constantly repeat the words, 'I should get rid of this disease,' 'I should get rid of this disease,' 'I should get rid of this disease,' you will constantly remember the disease also.

For example, if you have a headache, if you constantly think, 'I should get rid of this headache,' you give power to the headache as well.

In the epic *Ramayana* there is this character called Vali. Vali has a special power; he has a boon. Anybody who stands in front of him will lose half of their power to him. In the same way, when you repeat these words, 'I should get rid of this disease,' half of your power is given to the word 'disease.' You will never be successful. Create the right words, 'I should become healthy.' Without using the word disease, create the affirmation.

Try to be aware of the words that are going on inside you. Especially be aware of the words that you create unconsciously.

For example, early in the morning when you are brushing your teeth, you will be repeating some words inside you. When you are taking bath you will be constantly talking to yourself. Anybody here who says, 'No, I don't talk to myself when I am taking bath?' You may be singing, that's all. Either you will be singing or you will be talking to yourself. Constantly you will be talking to yourself within you, especially in the bathroom because nobody can hear you. Sometimes you will even start talking loudly.

Actually, it is a good practice to speak to yourself once in a while so that others will be liberated from having to listen to you! Otherwise you will catch people and constantly vomit on them.

Be very clear, nobody listens to you. They are polite so that once you stop they can start talking. Conversation never really happens. The other person is just waiting so that he can start speaking. The moment your voice is low, the moment you are slightly tired, the moment you are a little tired, immediately he gets hold of the microphone. Even when you are supposedly listening to the other person, you are just preparing your answer so that you can start once the other person stops. You are not actually listening. So once in a while, it is good for you to talk alone; you will spare others some grief.

The words which you speak when you are speaking to yourself when you are alone should be proper words. They should be the right words. Otherwise you will constantly be hurting yourself; you will be torturing yourself.

Here Ashtavakra says, *you are unattached.*

I was talking about the incident with the smoker. I told him either to drop smoking or to drop the guilt. He asked, 'How can I drop smoking by dropping the guilt? How can just dropping the guilt heal me?'

Please understand, in the morning this person smokes when he gets up from bed. Then after two hours, he smokes again. These two incidents are actually not as connected as they appear, they are unclutched. They are two separate incidents. But the guilt that he carries clutches both the incidents and makes both incidents appear connected.

Guilt - The Creator of the Pain Shaft

Please understand that I am speaking about the way in which your mind works. If you can understand this one truth, you can become unattached this moment. This moment you can become unclutched.

All your habits, all your activities, all your thoughts are disconnected, unclutched, individual incidents. However, by carrying guilt, pain, suffering, fear or worry about the habit, you make a shaft of thoughts that would otherwise not be there.

See, if the clutch in our car is not engaged (unclutched), our vehicle simply cannot move. Even if the engine is functioning, our vehicle cannot move. If the clutch is engaged or clutched, it starts moving. In our mind also, everything that is happening inside is completely unattached. They are individual, independent, separate incidents and separate happenings. The morning smoking and the afternoon smoking are two separate incidents; they are two different happenings. But the guilt clutches both the incidents and creates the shaft.

The shaft creates suffering for you through worry, guilt and fear. If you can have just a little bit of courage and drop these unnecessary fears, worries and guilt, you will realize that you are always unclutched.

Each and every statement or thought that is happening in your mind is completely unclutched. They are independent experiences. You cannot judge, connect or categorize them.

It is Never the 'Same'

Every single happening in our lives, even our everyday activities like eating and drinking are un-connected. Each and every experience is independent by its own right. Drinking yesterday and drinking today are two completely different incidents. Either through pain or through pleasure, you connect these two incidents. You then say that it is a habit and create a mind, which doesn't exist in reality. The food that you ate yesterday and the food which you eat today are different. You will not be able to eat the same food; fortunately you will not be able to do so. Only bats can eat the same food; bats vomit and eat the same food again.

The food that you ate yesterday and the food that you eat today are different; they are completely independent. But your mind creates the shaft between these two incidents and makes the whole thing as a single shaft and categorizes and says, 'I eat everyday.' Please be very clear, you don't eat the same food everyday. You may use the same word 'eating' for both the experiences but they are not the same experience. Do not be cheated by the words that you are using. Yesterday's eating, today's eating and tomorrow's eating are separate incidents, separate experiences. They are completely independent and unattached. But in your mind you start thinking, 'Oh, I eat the same food; I eat the same thing.'

When you are in a low mood, you constantly start connecting all these incidents. Either through pain or through pleasure, you connect them. Then you start saying, you start thinking, 'I am suffering' or 'I am enjoying.'

A beautiful incident from the life of an enlightened master from central India:

> During the last ten years of his life, the doctors had asked the master to eat a particular kind of food. He was not allowed to eat anything else. He was asked to eat the same kind of food daily.
>
> After two years the person who cooked for him came and complained, 'Master, I am bored with cooking the same food. How are you able to eat the same food day after day?'
>
> The master just laughed and said, 'I am not eating the same food every day. How can I eat the same food everyday? I can only eat *this* food today. Tomorrow's food is totally different.'

Your mind connects every independent incident, every independent thought with pain or pleasure. With your idea of pain or pleasure, you connect it. If your food is not right, you connect, 'Oh, same food, same suffering.'

> A wife who is stressed with her workload, tells the husband, 'If somebody sees my suffering, they will think you married me only for my cooking.'
>
> The husband replies, 'Not after eating your food!'

Unclutching is Your Very Nature

All your negativity has only one power; the faith that you place in it.

Whether it is your mind or your ego or whatever, all negativity has only one power, your faith in it. Understand that it is just a simple game.

You do not need to work for unclutching. Just do not clutch and do not create a shaft.

People tell me again and again, '*Swamiji*, I fail when I try to unclutch.' I ask them, 'Why are you connecting your past failure with your present failure?' When you connect all the past failures, you create one more word 'failure'. Why do you connect all of them and create the next experience also?

Just relax and stop connecting and suddenly you will see such a deep inner healing happening in you, such a deep peace happening in you. Suddenly you will see that you have dropped out of the war, the constant running. Just relax.

I tell you, when you become a dropout, when you drop out of this war, when you drop from this whole game, you will suddenly realize the whole thing is just a psychodrama happening. Because you constantly support it, you connect the incidents through pain or pleasure and create these shafts.

Be very clear:

Because of your memory of pain or pleasure, you think you have a constant mind and a continuous thought flow.

Please understand, I am not saying that tomorrow or day after tomorrow or after your enlightenment, you will become unattached. No! You *are* unattached this very moment. Simply this moment, you *are* unattached.

The thought that appeared in your mind one minute ago and the thought that is appearing now are not connected. These two are complete, independent thoughts.

If you had some experience of pleasure as you think, whenever those kinds of incidents are

repeated, immediately you connect that pleasure and this pleasure.

Understand, by the time you connect that pleasure and this pleasure, you have created a shaft. Now you are trying to fight with the shaft. If you think the shaft is painful, you want to break the shaft. If you think the shaft is pleasure, you want to extend the shaft. But you can neither break the shaft nor extend the shaft, because the shaft does not exist.

Just understand that there is no such thing as continuity between one thought and another thought. You are unattached now.

You do not have to practice renunciation. Your very nature is renunciation.

Whatever happens in you, you are constantly renouncing; you are constantly replacing yourself. Only if one thought is renounced, another thought can arise, is it not? So at every moment when a thought appears in you, whether it is fulfilled or unfulfilled, you

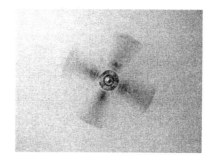
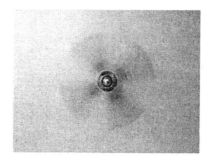

Just like a fan with independent blades while in rapid motion creates the optical illusion of continuity, so also our independent thoughts rapidly arising one after the other create the illusion of the mind

actually renounce that thought. Only then the next thought can come up. All you need to do is allow the constant renunciation happening in you. This moment, just by this very understanding you can unclutch yourself.

Why Cull from the Garbage Can?

Here is another way to look at this process: you are constantly discarding your e-mails in the trash bin. After that, you suddenly pick up an email from your trash and clutch with it.

Similarly, all your thoughts are going to the trash every moment. But suddenly you pick up some from the trash, try to clutch them, and create a shaft. Just stop picking up thoughts from your garbage bin, nothing else is needed. Just leave the garbage bin alone; the city will come and clean it! But you do not feel comfortable. After ten minutes you run to the garbage and pick up couple of things saying, 'I think this is nice. I will keep it near my bed.' After one hour you run again and pick up one more thought, 'I think this is nicer.' You collect more and more trash and put it next to your bed, add a little perfume and try to keep it looking nice. You try to decorate it and feel good about it.

Understand, you are constantly discarding or throwing away your thoughts. This is why new thoughts are appearing. The very truth that new thoughts are happening in you means that the old thoughts have been renounced. The appearance of new thoughts means that the old thoughts have disappeared. So do not be afraid to throw away the old thoughts. Do not be greedy by retrieving them, clutching them, and creating a shaft.

Your knowledge about your past plays a major role in creating your future. Be very clear about your past. Here I am analyzing how you create an identity about yourself. This is the identity about yourself. This pain

shaft is an identity about yourself which you are constantly creating. You may think, 'Once a month I fall sick,' 'Once in two or three days I will be in a low mood,' 'If I work until after eight o'clock I will get irritated.' You strongly believe in the pain shaft. These shafts create all the conflicts, all the disturbances in your life. Even your physical health is terribly disturbed by these shafts.

In the same way, you create a joy shaft and create an identity about yourself.

Are 'You' Needed to Run Your Life?

You think that unless you carry your identity, you cannot protect yourself. But that identity which you carry does not really exist.

The moment I say that your identity is a lie, a tremendous fear rises in you, 'If I unclutch, who will take care of my life? Who will take care of my day-to-day living?' Be very clear, you need to understand a very important truth. Even though it hurts, it is the truth.

We have an automatic intelligence in us that constantly runs our lives. For example, do you mentally plan your drive back to your house? While you drive you have to do so many things including: using the clutch, pressing the accelerator, looking at the directions, looking at the traffic or respecting the traffic signals, to name a few. If you have to mentally create a plan for each of these like, 'I have to take my key and turn the key, start the car, turn 20 degrees to the right, 30 degrees to the left, press the accelerator once, press the brake once, look at the traffic in the front and stop for the signal', if you have to plan verbally, and if you have to do the whole thing in your mind, will you be able to drive? No!

You are able to drive without creating all these words in you, is it not? Not only that, your car is your restaurant where you have your breakfast everyday! It is your club for listening to music, it is your phone booth to make your phone calls, and so on. You drive, you take care of the traffic, you listen to the music and you talk on the cellphone.

Understand one important thing:

We have an automatic intelligence which can run our lives, which can take care of our day-to-day life. Not only can it run our lives, it can maintain, it can extend or expand our lives.

Just as you do not need your mind while driving, you do not need your planning, you do not need your mind to run your day-to-day life as well. Many times you get into the car at home and when you stop the car at the office parking lot, suddenly you realize you have finished driving that entire distance, is it not? From your house to your office, you would not have had a single thought about your driving. Suddenly when you stop your car, you will come to know that you have finished driving. You have traveled many miles without even a single thought that you are driving or without any thoughts related to driving. This shows that there is an automatic intelligence in you.

The *vedic* science says that there is an automatic, programmed intelligence in us which can run and expand our lives and energy. This is a revealing and an important truth. Please understand that you are not needed to run your life. What you think of as you is not needed to run your life. Again and again *vedic* masters are revealing this truth; the Eastern *rishis* are expressing this truth.

Your constant psychological planning, psychological worrying, fears, greed, whatever you think of as you, is not needed to run your life. Your very automatic intelligence is more than enough.

But, society conditions you from a young age. You are taught to think that you cannot run without planning, that you cannot run without fear or greed. Your self-respect is taken away from you. You are not made to

trust that you can lead your life spontaneously without fear or greed. You are always trained to think that you can run only with fear or greed. That is why constantly you are trying to infuse greed or fear into yourself. You try to use fear and greed as fuel to make your life run, to make your life alive.

Be very clear that you cannot run your life based on fear and greed.

If you are driven by fear and greed, you will carry a constant irritation in you.

From morning until night, from the moment you wake up to the moment you go to sleep, you will carry a constant irritation in you. That is why you are just waiting for a reason to explode. You are waiting for some reason to vomit. Just one small touch is enough, and you are ready to jump on the other person. He does not even need to make any mistake; just coming in front of you is enough to trigger you. Coming into your presence is enough; you just pounce on the other person.

Any simple reason is enough. The wife placing a coffee cup down with a little force, a little sound is enough for the husband to start shouting at her, 'What! Do you think you have brought all these things from your father's house? I have worked hard for it.' Then she starts, 'You are lucky to get even coffee for the job that you are doing. Keep quiet and drink!' Then the whole drama starts. You know what the next statement will be; I don't have to tell you! The constant irritation is in you because you try to fuel yourself by fear or greed.

Surrender to Your Higher Intelligence

Neither fear nor greed can make your life run smoothly. When you unclutch, suddenly you realize that you are not needed to run your life. When you can drive without using your mind, why can't you live your life this way? You can. Trusting the automatic intelligence within you is all you need to do;

then relax. That is what we call in Sanskrit as *sharanagati* - surrender. The English translation would be 'surrendering to your own higher intelligence'.

Please understand, 'Surrendering to your own higher intelligence'. When the Eastern *rishis* say surrender, they mean surrendering to our own higher intelligence. Only when we surrender to our own higher intelligence, we can surrender to God. Surrendering to the higher intelligence is what we call surrendering to God.

When you surrender and let go of the identities that you carry, *ahankar* and *mamakar*, you will feel a tremendous freedom.

If you understand that both the identities are not needed to live your life, to run your life, to run, protect and expand your life, you will suddenly realize a tremendous freedom. You can be alive without these two identities.

Freedom from these two identities is what I call liberation, enlightenment, *moksha* and *nirvana*. Whatever words you may use, it is nothing but liberation from these two identities.

These two identities are the bondage. When you understand that you are something beyond these two identities, you are *jeevan mukta*, liberated while living. What you think as you is not necessary to be alive. I tell you, if you drop what you think of as you, only then you will become alive. Until then, you will be living, inhaling and exhaling, breathing, but never think you are alive. Breathing is not a symptom of living; never think you are alive living this way.

Just because you have a key to your house, do not think it is your home; it is a tomb. We are all waiting for death, not living. There are two categories of people: one is living and another one is waiting for death. We are just waiting for death. We do not have the courage to commit suicide; so we are just waiting for death to happen by itself.

Jeevan Mukti - Relaxing from *ahankar* and *mamakar*

Living means freedom from the two identities, one that you carry inside yourself, *mamakar* and the one that you project to the outer world, *ahankar*. When we relax from these two, we achieve what is called *jeevan mukti*.

We do not even need to relax from them because new thoughts are constantly replacing them. The moment the next thought has appeared, we have renounced the earlier thought. Every moment we are renouncing thoughts. Every moment, we are getting unattached. Every moment we are constantly replacing all our thoughts.

If you think you are tortured by your fears, you are wrong. If you think you are tortured by your greed, you are wrong. We are neither tortured by our fears, nor are we tortured by our greed because every thought is constantly getting replaced with a fresh thought. The thought that you are getting tortured is the only actual torture for you.

If you feel, 'I am getting tortured at this moment,' try to understand it is the thought that is torturing you, that's all. Do not believe it will come back. By believing it will come back, the belief itself will bring it back.

Even if you have a strong desire, a strong greed, another single thought can just replace that greed. One single thought can replace fear. Then, how can desire and greed be strong?

You cannot be a follower unless you carry some suffering.

If you do not carry suffering, you will become a leader. Leaders are dangerous people. That is why society never wants you to be independent, creative and alive - a leader. Be very clear, a leader will be a person who is creative, who is expressing, who is on his own. However, society does not want that.

It is very difficult to handle a leader. It is easy to handle followers. It is easy to handle masses if they are kept as followers. That is why the great wisdom, the great truth – 'By your very nature you are unclutched', is kept a secret. It is kept a secret because if you understand this truth, you cannot be exploited; there is no way you can be exploited.

I always tell people that the only thing self-development programs accomplish is to give you 'feel-good feelings.' Your self cannot develop, because it does not exist. When it doesn't exist, where is the question of developing it? If the shaft exists, then you could chisel it, polish it, rub it, paint it, goldplate it and keep it. But the shaft itself does not exist. What will you then develop? Even if you try to develop the shaft, it will be nothing but taking something that you have discarded, arranging it properly, adding a little perfume and trying to feel the scent, nothing else. Understand that you are constantly throwing your thoughts away in the trash, so there is no shaft in reality.

Be very clear, what you think as you or self is nothing but the discarded thoughts including the randomly picked, unconnected, illogical and unclutched thoughts. You pick from these, create a shaft and think you are those thoughts and try to develop a self which does not exist.

I worked to develop myself for one year. Understand, all these techniques, whether they are spiritual practices or self-development practices, are all trying to create a consistent shaft in you. When you say something is good or something is bad, you start becoming greedy for the good and fearful about the bad. You start encouraging one and suppressing the other.

The moment you choose to do either, you have created a problem for yourself. Now whatever you suppress will be constantly coming up in your mind. Whatever you want will constantly disappear from your mind.

A small story:

> A young *brahmachari* goes to a senior 90 year old monk and asks him, 'Swamiji, I am suffering with too many bad thoughts. Too many bad thoughts are coming to my mind. How long do I have to suffer before getting rid of these bad, dirty thoughts?'
>
> The senior elderly monk looks this side and that side and says, 'I don't know how long it takes, but one thing is sure, it doesn't happen until you are at least ninety!'

Whatever you are avoiding is going to exist in you. Whatever you are trying to encourage is going to be disconnected. You can neither break a shaft nor can you elongate it because the shaft does not exist.

Identity - The Biggest Lie In Your Life

Because your life needs an identity, because you need an identity, you are always afraid. If I say that you are inconsistent, by your very nature you are illogical, unconnected, and unclutched, you feel a tremendous fear rising in you. People ask me again and again, 'How can we live without the mind? How can we live without identity?'

Be very clear, your identity has convinced you. Your mind has convinced you by showing you a few examples that you cannot be alive without it, that you cannot survive without it. It is like if you convince your boss that he cannot run his business without you, you can do whatever you want. You can exploit him.

In the same way, your mind has convinced you by giving a few examples. A long time ago you would have made some mistakes and something might have happened in your life as a result of those mistakes. Your mind will constantly show them to you and tell you, 'See, you did not listen to me, that is why it happened. You did not follow my planning, that is why it happened. You did not follow up, you did not plan, and you did not worry about execution. You did not execute, that is why it happened.'

It will constantly show you those few incidents and convince you that you need to have a mind. Once you are convinced that you cannot be alive without your identity, your mind will exploit you. Now your identity will swallow your whole life.

There will be continuous conflict between the two identities that you carry; that is what I call mobile hell! Wherever you go you carry them just like how you carry your tent when you go camping. In the same way you carry your mobile hell. Whether you go to the beach or anywhere else on vacation, you carry your mobile hell with you. The continuous conflict between the two identities is tension.

Please try to understand these few concepts. You have two identities, one is based on inferiority and the other one is based on superiority. There is a continuous conflict between these two, which is what is called 'tension'. The next important truth is that you are beyond these two identities.

Be very clear, if you just understand these few concepts intellectually, even the experience of eating will be transformed for you; even the taste as well as the sensitivity in your body will be transformed. The sensitivity will be awakened once you understand that you are beyond these two identities. These two identities limit you, put you in boundaries, do not allow you to update yourself. Updating yourself is not possible if you put boundaries which are based on these two identities.

Only when you understand that you are beyond these two identities, the two identities cannot disturb you. You can get out of suffering only when you relax by

understanding that you are beyond these two identities. If you want to heal your life physically, mentally or emotionally, the one and only way is realizing that you are beyond these two identities, because all of your problems are related to only these two identities and conflict between these two identities. Unless you realize that you are beyond them, you cannot experience the balance or the silence or the peace or bliss in your life.

How to Unclutch from the Identities?

The *vedic* masters have created a beautiful formula to reproduce the same experience in you that happened in them. The experience that you are beyond these two identities happened in them and they created a formula to reproduce the same in you. It is that formula that I call 'Be unclutched'.

Now the next question is, how to unclutch? Let us first understand how we clutch, how we connect. Only then we can understand how we can unclutch. Only if you understand how the knot is created can you remove it. If you do not know how the knot is created, you cannot undo it. You will be just pulling, pulling and pulling and what will happen? The knot will only tighten more. We are doing just that as of now.

Just like the knot, the conflict between these two identities exists and we are pulling from both sides, each side representing a different identity.

Either you are trying to satisfy the identity that is working in the outer world, making more and more money, making the identity which you show to the outer world bigger and bigger, having more wealth and bigger things, or you enter the other side, trying to do different types of religious practices.

You can neither pull from this direction nor can you pull from that direction. If you try to pull in either direction the knot will only get tighter.

Understand how you created the knot. Understand the depth of the knot and how you created the knot. Only then you can get out of the knot. Only then you can unclutch.

Here Ashtavakra says: *You are unattached.* When Ashtavakra says, *you are unattached,* he means that there is no shaft. There is no shaft; there are simply independent thoughts. Independent, unconnected, illogical thoughts appear separately and disappear. Because of your idea about pain or pleasure, you connect these thoughts and create a shaft and feel as if there is a shaft. Just understand this very moment that the shaft does not exist, and be liberated.

Constantly, you are unattached. Automatically, by your very nature, you are unattached. The moment that you understand that you are unattached, you are just liberated. A tremendous inner healing starts happening in you. A tremendous sense of rest happens in you. You will think, 'Oh God, what have I been fighting for? I was fighting with a person who does not even exist. All my energy was wasted. It was wasted unnecessarily fighting with a person who doesn't exist.' Your idea of pain, pleasure or ego does not exist. Simply, it is not there.

In the *vedic* system we say *kshana. Kshana* does not mean 'one second' as it is generally thought. *Kshana* means the gap between one thought and the other thought. Between one thought and another thought, we drop into the *atman*. There is no connection between one thought and another thought. The moment you understand that there is no connection between one thought and another thought, you drop into the source of thoughts, from where all the thoughts appear. You go to the source and come back.

You can just unclutch yourself this very moment. Relax from the fighting. But a tremendous fear rises, 'If I stop fighting, then how will I develop my life?' It is only when you stop fighting, the transformation can happen. Be very clear, the mind can never be

developed. Either you keep this mind and suffer, or drop this mind and transform yourself. There are only two choices available to you, either mind or no mind. Developing your mind is not an option because it is just not possible to develop your mind.

Just Let Go...And You Can Fly!

I will just give a simple example to show how you are tortured by your identity, how you suffer with your identity. This will show how you are afraid to unclutch yourself, why you are not ready to unclutch yourself, why you are just not opening up and understanding this truth.

In the forests of Northern India, hunters use a trap to catch birds. They tie a rope between two trees. In the middle of the rope they secure a wooden stick. The rope is tied at the midpoint of the stick. This is actually a hunter's trap for birds.

You may think, 'How can a bird be trapped with a small stick? How is it possible?' Actually, all they do is just hang the stick, that's all. When a bird comes and sits on the stick, by the bird's own weight, the whole stick will turn upside down; it will turn topsy-turvy. Now, the bird will also be hanging upside down.

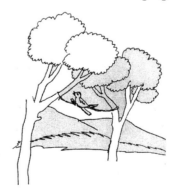

The bird is so afraid that if it lets go of the stick, it will fall and die. The poor bird does not know that if it lets go of the stick, it can simply fly. It starts thinking that if it relaxes, it will fall and die; it will fall and break its head.

Understand, by the bird's own weight, the stick turns topsy-turvy, upside down. Once it becomes upside down, the poor bird starts thinking, 'If I let go, I may fall and break my head, I may fall and hurt myself, I may fall and just die.' So it just hangs and hangs there for hours together.

After one or two hours, the hunter slowly comes and puts it in his bag and takes it away. The bird does not know and he does not have the intelligence to realize that if he just relaxes, if he lets go, he can just fly! At the most it may

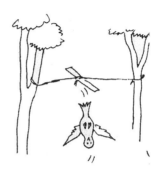

take one or two moments to balance, that's all. Have you ever heard of a bird falling and dying? No!

There is no record of a single bird falling and dying. There is no record that any bird fell and broke its head. But the bird does not have the intelligence to realize that. It keeps hanging on.

The poor bird hangs upside down, holding on to the stick, thinking it will fall and die if it lets go. However, by not letting go, not only does it lose its freedom, it loses its life too. Just like

that foolish bird, you are also thinking that you can be alive only with your identity.

You do not understand that if you let go of your identity, you can become a Paramahamsa, a great swan; you can just fly! Just like the bird which does not know that it can fly only if it lets go, you also do not know, that you can become enlightened if you relax from your identity. The poor bird holding on to the stick for security not only misses its freedom, when the hunter comes the bird will be taken away from that stick as well.

In the same way, you hold on to whatever you think is your identity and security - your education, your mind, your life, your relationships, or your bank balance. By holding on to these, not only do you lose your freedom, not only do you lose your enlightenment, but when *Yamadharma*, the Lord of Death arrives, you lose even the stick that you are holding onto for security. Even that will be taken away from you.

So understand, what you think of as security is not security. It is a prison. You think your identity is your security. You think that it is protecting you, just like how the bird thinks that the stick is protecting it. Be very clear, your fear and the bird's fear are one and the same. The bird does not know that if it relaxes, it can fly; it can escape and have his freedom. In the same way, you do not understand that if you have the courage and let go, if you have the courage and open yourself, you can simply fly; you will be a Paramahamsa!

Please understand this one thing: just like how the bird is not able to trust, how the bird is not able to understand that by letting go or opening up it can fly, you also suffer. You are also afraid, 'If I stop connecting all my experiences in a linear way, if I stop connecting the incidents of my life with pain or pleasure, I may constantly suffer, I may fall into pain, people may exploit me... How will I maintain my bank balance? How will I maintain my house? How will I extract work from my subordinates?' You have one thousand fears just like the bird.

Please understand, I am telling this to you from my own experience. I was also holding on like that. I was also holding on just like you.

Let me tell you:
Simply let go; you will fly. You will simply fly. Understand this moment that you are unattached.

Just like how the birds are hanging until the hunter comes and takes them away, you are also waiting for Yama, the Lord of Death. Of course, when he comes, you will have to let go of whatever you are holding onto and he will help you to let go. Please understand, do not wait for Yama to come. Just let go, just open up. You can simply fly like a bird. You are unattached.

If you realize this truth, your enlightenment is guaranteed.

Realize this truth and be liberated. Be established and be in eternal bliss, *nithyananda*.

Questions and answers

Q: How can we leave everything and survive here in this world? We need to make an effort. We need to make a living. How can one do that?

A: Nice question. When you drive, do you plan every step, do you raise the word drive...

Q: At this point, we have a lot of practice driving - we drive, drive and drive.

A: In the same way you are trained to be alive.

Q: No. Alive is one thing, but one needs to earn a living, one needs to make an effort.

A: Do you know how to breathe? You are programmed for breathing. Let me tell you clearly from my experience and even *vedic rishis* have said again and again, that if your body is programmed to breathe, your body is programmed to make your living also.

Q: Can I just sit here and earn my bread and butter?

A: First thing, you will not be able to sit here like that. Try to be unclutched. You will have an intelligence which is simply making your body move and work. Be very clear, the moment I say unclutch, you associate it with laziness. You have a deep hatred towards working, that is the reason. So you go towards the opposite direction of resting or being lazy.

See, the moment I say unclutch, you think of just lying down on the bed. But you will not be able to just lie down on your bed. Try to unclutch and suddenly you will see that so much of creativity is expressed through you. So much intelligence will happen through you. You will not become lazy. Be very clear, you will not become lazy.

I talked about the bird earlier. Understand, if that bird has a little intelligence and flies, relaxes and balances, the bird will know how to escape from the clutch, the trap. Then the same trap will become a hammock for the bird! It can just come and swing; it can come and sit on the same rope and use it like a hammock. The same trap will be a hammock for the bird.

In the same way, when you unclutch from your identity and fly, you will know how to handle your identity. Now your identity will not be a prison anymore. It will become a hammock for you!

Do not think if you unclutch, you will not practice your profession or you will not do your job. If you are a doctor, do not think that if you unclutch, you will not be able to perform as a competent doctor. If you unclutch, there will be only one difference. You will not have the constant irritation which you carry in your life from morning till night. Whatever profession you are in, the deep irritation, vengeance and arrogance that you carry will be expressed in your body language, in your words, in your step. That is what you are expressing in your body language, in your words, in your questions, in your steps.

If you have a little intelligence, I can tell you, just try this simple experiment.

Try to be unclutched just for ten days. Surely in ten days I do not think you will lose your job. Will you lose all your wealth in just ten days? Surely you must have savings enough for ten days. Try to be unclutched just for ten days. Suddenly you will see that you are not able to be lazy. The tremendous energy that you are wasting in psychological worrying and irritation, will become creative energy. Then, you will not work hard, but you will work smart.

Understand, a clutched person works hard, an unclutched person works smart. Even your idea of doing hard work is a pure myth because of clutching.

What is hard work? Before doing simple work, if you plan psychologically ten times, worry whether it will happen or not ten more times, and after completing it, if you talk and brag about it ten more times, it will become hard work. Hard work is nothing but doing some small, simple work, talking about it ten times, planning about it ten times, worrying about whether it will happen or not ten times and after doing it, bragging about it. Otherwise whatever you call hard work is pure myth, done out of arrogance.

Be very clear, I am not sitting quietly. I am not a lazy *swami* or a lazy monk in the Himalayas. I travel one hundred thousand miles per year and I run eight hundred centers in twenty-four countries. Let me tell you honestly, just because of unclutching, so much of creativity and power is being expressed. As of now you waste 90% of your energy in psychological worrying. When I say 90% I mean 90%.

When your ego is hurt, you try to defend your philosophy. Please be very clear about what I say; your ego is hurt. Have a little intelligence and look in and be a new being. Just take ten days, not more than that. Drop your hard work myth. You feel important only if you feel you are doing hard work.

In the initial level you have to convince your boss that you are doing hard work. By and by you yourself get convinced that you are doing hard work. Hard work is the ultimate myth.

Let me be very clear, you are not doing hard work at all. That is the first thing you need to understand. You keep on telling your kids, 'I did this for you, I did that for you,' so that you can create guilt in them and make them do what you want them to.

Actually one father and son came to me. The father said, 'I did this for him. I did that for him. He is not obeying me Master, please tell him.' The son asked me, 'Master, who asked him to give birth to me? He did something and I happened as a by-product of that. After the son is born, he goes on saying, 'I did this and I did that for you.'

Be very clear, we do not do anything for anybody. Not just for others, but also even for ourselves. Hard work is pure myth. Let us understand this simple fact and try just for ten days. For ten days, just try to be unclutched. You will see the amount of energy and creativity that comes out of you and expresses through you. You will not be able to keep quiet. Just unclutch; you will not work hard but you will work smart.

Q: My question is why do we have questions in the first place if we are unclutched?

A: Nice question. First thing let us analyze two things. If you understand that you are unclutched, you will not have questions. If you have questions, at that moment you are not unclutched. You are trying to clutch on to something.

If you look in and understand that you are unclutched, naturally you will not have any questions. Where is the question of having questions? You will not have any thoughts. Just look and see that you are unclutched by your very nature.

*Enlightenment –
              Have It!!!*

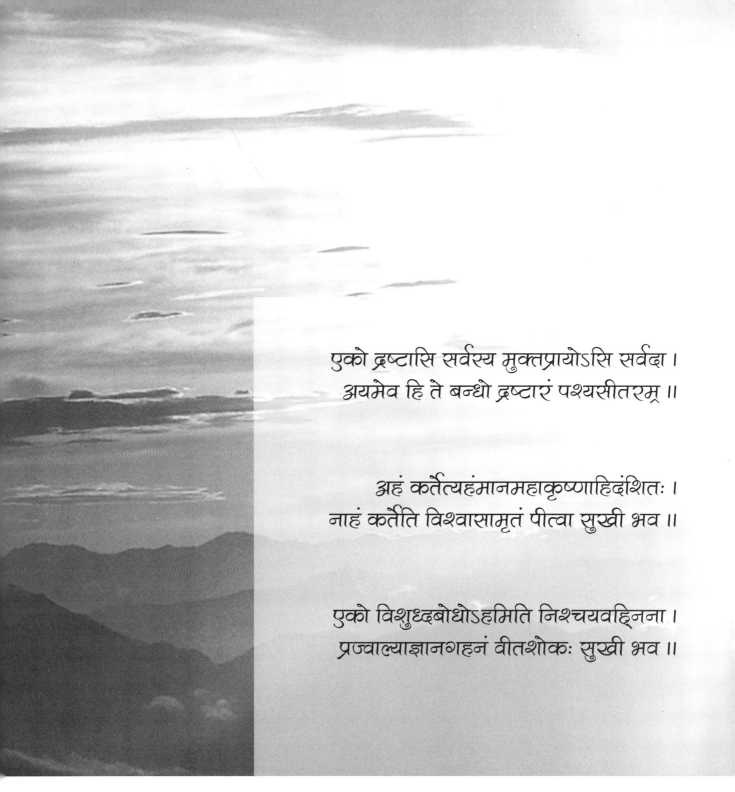

एको द्रष्टासि सर्वस्य मुक्तप्रायोऽसि सर्वदा।
अयमेव हि ते बन्धो द्रष्टारं पश्यसीतरम्॥

अहं कर्तेत्यहंमानमहाकृष्णाहिदंशितः।
नाहं कर्तेति विश्वासामृतं पीत्वा सुखी भव॥

एको विशुद्धबोधोऽहमिति निश्चयवह्निना।
प्रज्वाल्याज्ञानगहनं वीतशोकः सुखी भव॥

Chapter 3

You are the one seer of all and really ever free.
Verily this alone is your bondage
that you see the seer as other than such.

You who have been bitten by the great black serpent of egoism
'I am the doer'
Drink the nectar of the faith,
'I am not the doer' and be happy.

Burn down the wilderness of ignorance
with the fire of the knowledge,
I am the one and pure intelligence
And be free from grief and be happy.

Today's topic is Enlightenment – Have it!!! On the first day, we saw a few basic things about enlightenment based on *Ashtavakra Gita*: Enlightenment - It Is Possible! The next day, we understood a few things from Enlightenment – Guaranteed!! Now today, it is Enlightenment – Have it!!!

By Very Nature, You Renounce Every Moment

Let us enter into the *sutra* and see how Ashtavakra says that we can simply have it. He also shows us how to have it:

Virtue and vice, pleasure and pain are of the mind, not of you.

Oh all-pervading one, you are neither doer nor enjoyer.
Verily you are ever free.

In this *sutra*, Ashtavakra directly addresses Janaka as the all-pervading one. Here he directly says to Janaka, *'Oh, all-pervading one.'* Until this point he was saying, 'You are this, you are that, you are pure consciousness.' Now he straightaway addresses Janaka as *all-pervading one*.

Virtue and vice, pleasure and pain are of the mind, not of you.

Actually, Ashtavakra is answering the doubts that will come after listening to the truth of being unattached. Yesterday, I talked about how there is no shaft in our being. We are completely un-clutched. Every moment, by our nature, we renounce our thoughts. Unless we renounce one thought, we cannot have the next thought. By our very nature, we are constantly renouncing our thoughts.

Only fools try to create the same thoughts over and over again. Whether you try to visualize or verbalize the same things constantly, this can be harmful to you. Please be very clear, the Eastern consciousness is suffering because you are constantly trying to visualize or verbalize something.

Almost all the people who take up spiritual life try one exercise or another. They are constantly trying to visualize something or verbalize something through some *mantra* or some form of technique. Both visualizing and verbalizing can work against you. By our very nature we are unattached. By our very nature we renounce thoughts. The more we try to stay with one thought, the more we suffer.

I have seen people who try to chant some *mantra* or use some visualization technique for thirty or forty years. After forty years they come to me and ask me, 'Master, how can I learn to concentrate? Please teach me how to concentrate.' To tell you honestly, I do not know, because that situation never happened to me. I have seen thousands of seekers constantly trying to repeat a thought or to repeat the same *mantra* or to bring the same visualization in their minds. Unfortunately, they never succeeded with this approach. In the end, they became completely frustrated and failed in achieving the result that they were seeking.

After that failure, they tried to find other solutions. Please understand, by our very nature, we are constantly renouncing thoughts. Unless we renounce one thought, we cannot go to the next thought. The moment we renounce one thought, we go to the next thought. By our very nature we are renouncing thoughts.

If we try to keep our mind focused on a single thought, we will only be torturing ourselves. I have seen people torturing themselves through some *mantra* or some visualization. But whether it is *mantra* or visualization, both create only more and more pressure and stress in us.

By repeating words or *mantras*, the only thing that you can do is attempt to create a consistent shaft. These efforts to create a consistent shaft will not be successful because it is not possible to create a consistent shaft. I have tried it myself in my own life and I can tell you that it is impossible. If you are in the habit of repeating some syllable or some word or *mantra*, you will understand what I mean. You will be just waiting and thinking, 'When will I finish this?' You will be waiting to finish it. In the same way, if you are trying to avoid something, you will see it constantly surface and you will be fighting with it.

You already have enough pain and problems. Now you create one more pain of repeating some *mantra* or creating some visualization. Be very clear, by your very nature you cannot be with the same thought continuously. You cannot be with just one thought for a significant period of time. All you need to understand is that by your very nature, you are unattached. Just as Ashtavakra says in the *sutra*, '*By your very nature you are unattached.*'

Thoughts are Like Bubbles in A Fish Tank

There is no linear connection between one thought and another thought within us. The only relationship between thoughts is that they come from the same source.

The moment you hear this truth you are shocked because you are constantly connecting one thought and the next thought in a linear manner.

For example, you will connect the depression that you are experiencing today with the depression that you experienced yesterday. The moment you connect the independent incidents that have happened in your life, you start creating an idea that you are a depressed being. Also, if you connect all joyful incidents of your life, you come to the conclusion that you are a joyful being. You come up with  some concept about yourself by connecting all your thoughts in a linear way.

Just like the bubbles in a fish tank come up from the bottom, your thoughts also rise in the same manner. When one bubble comes and reaches the surface of the water, the next bubble starts and then the third bubble starts. You start connecting all these bubbles on the surface of the water.

Because of your memory of pain or pleasure, you start connecting all the bubbles and start thinking that your mind is linear. No, your mind is not linear. In order to move from one bubble to the next you cannot move horizontally; you can go only vertically. Every bubble is coming from the *atman*, soul, your being.

Connecting Your Thoughts - The Original Sin

One big problem is that you do not connect *all* your thoughts. Instead you choose just a few thoughts and connect them. Some people feel that their whole life is pain and some people feel that their whole life is joy.

When you connect your thoughts in a selective linear manner, you create an idea that your whole life is pain or your whole life is joy or pleasure. If you feel that your whole life is pain, you will try to break the shaft.

If you feel that your whole life is pleasure, you will try to extend that shaft. Either way, you will fail. You will be a complete and utter failure with this effort because there actually is no shaft.

Connecting and seeing your thoughts in a linear way is the original sin that you commit. Creating the shaft in your mind is the original sin.

In doing so, you are creating something inside you that does not exist - the mind.

Mind is a pure myth.

Somehow we have learned the habit of keeping files. I have seen people keeping files, not only about themselves but about others as well.

> Let me tell you about an incident, which happened during one of my visits:
>
> One gentleman around forty–five years of age came up to me and said, 'Master, I am going to divorce my wife, please bless me.'
>
> I told him, 'I only bless individuals for marriages. What made you come and ask me to bless you for a divorce?' He replied, 'No, no Master, you have to bless me, because I have suffered too much.'

I said, 'Suffering is always give and take. It is never just taking. You must have given her enough suffering too. So please tell me the truth about what happened and then we will analyze the situation.'

But again he said, 'No, no, Master, you don't know how much I have suffered. You are a *swami*, so you don't know about all these things.'

I said, 'Please do not attack me directly! Just tell me a few incidents. Then we will come to some understanding.'

To this he replied, 'Which ones do you want me to tell, and which ones do you want me to leave out? From day one she has been torturing me. You do not know how much of torture I have gone through!'

In Indian villages, when a wedding takes place, the newly married couple plays games after the ceremony. For one of the games, a ring is placed inside a pot filled with water. The husband and wife put their hands inside and compete to pick up the ring. Whoever grabs it first wins. These small games were created mainly to reduce the distance between the couple, because in arranged marriages it was only during the wedding ceremony that the couple first met. They have small games to reduce the distance between the couple because they are new to each other.

This man said, 'During that game, she scratched my hand. With her nails, she scratched my hand, Master.' And he started a big story about everything that she supposedly had done to him since that day. For all practical purposes, he had kept a file, like a police report from the first day of his marriage.

After two or three incidents were narrated I told him, 'Please stop! If this is the case, she should be happier than you to part ways. It is very difficult to live with someone who keeps such large and detailed files in their head!' Any time she does something, this man will always be looking through the files.

For example, he told me the immediate reason for the divorce was that she spilled some coffee on his clothes! I replied to him, 'Spilling coffee on the clothes cannot be a reason for a divorce. You cannot give me such insignificant reasons for divorcing your wife.'

To that his response was, 'No, no Master, you don't know. Today she poured coffee; tomorrow she will pour acid!' He really said this. I did not understand the connection. I asked him how he could possibly connect coffee and acid. Again he said, 'No, no Master you don't know.'

Then I told him, 'Look at the incidents as independent incidents. She brought you the coffee and she spilled a little bit on your clothes by mistake. In any case, she is probably the one who washes your clothes. You are probably not even going to wash it yourself. It was just an independent incident. But when you have a huge file, when you have a huge case history, before passing judgment about a small incident, you just verify the whole file. In two or three seconds you verify the whole file and then you start shouting. Then you start creating words in your mind that today she poured coffee and tomorrow she will pour acid. You start creating big statements in your mind.'

Please understand, when I mentioned that he said, 'Today she will pour coffee and tomorrow she will pour acid', you all laughed. But you all are also doing the same thing in your own lives! You are constantly creating a connection which is illogical. You forget to see incidents as independent. You

forget to see thoughts as independent. By your very nature, you have only independent thoughts. All your thoughts are completely independent.

If you just learn this one simple technique of un-clutching, you will release a significant amount of the energy in your system, in your being. As a result, you will be ten times more productive and more creative. Your relationships will have much more friendliness because you will not clutch to incidents that are not related.

Collecting Arguments to Support Your Judgments

At this point, you don't trust the other person. You cannot believe that you or your spouse has become intelligent in the last few years. You never sincerely trust that he or she has grown and become intelligent because you never trust that you yourself could grow and become intelligent.

You will be maintaining the same idea that you had formed about him or her ten years ago. No matter what your spouse does, you will only look at him or her through the same lens. Whatever he does, she will think, 'He never listens to me.' Whatever she does, he will say, 'She tries to boss me around.' You have this preconceived idea.

That is why I tell people, you always live with the other person for six months, and in six months, you create an idea about the other person. Once you create an idea about the other person, it's over. The man will create the idea, 'I don't have to go to hell after death because the punishment is given now.' And the woman will create the idea, 'God has sent me this as punishment; I have to finish all my *karmas*.' Both create similar ideas. After that whatever he or she does, the other looks at their actions only through that coloured lens.

You never un-clutch from your ideas or your prejudices. You do not listen to arguments before passing judgments or reconsider a judgment that you have made. You only collect arguments to support your own judgments. The judgment is already there and you are just waiting for arguments in support of it. Whenever you find a solid argument, you catch hold of it and support your judgment.

Your Mind is Illogical, Unconnected, Unclutched Thoughts

If you do a very simple experiment for just ten minutes then you will understand this better. Sit alone and write down whatever is going on in your mind. Do not edit, do not suppress any thoughts. It is an experiment only for you. Do not show it to anyone else, at least not to your family members. Visualize that a transcribing software has been connected to your mind. Just like how the transcribing software which is connected to a taped speech transcribes everything, you transcribe whatever is going on in your mind verbatim.

Write down everything. You may think, 'Oh, nothing is coming to my mind.' Write down this statement as well; this is also one more thought. Whatever goes on, just write it down for a period of ten minutes. At the end of ten minutes, read what you wrote only once. You will understand that inside you is a big, mad asylum.

You will understand how every thought is completely illogical, irresponsible and unconnected, how you are completely un-clutched. For example you are sitting here and suddenly you will get thoughts such as, 'Why don't I take a month's vacation? No, why don't I go home and do some work? I think I should go to this Swami's ashram and see what he does. Can I go tomorrow?

He is still not finished and I am hungry. What is happening?'

You can see how everything is flowing in your mind. Actually if you do this exercise just once, you will understand how unconnected, illogical, independent and un-clutched those thoughts are. This understanding can be so transforming. This very understanding transforms the way that you think about yourself and your way of conducting yourself with others and with yourself. It just transforms your whole life.

When you read what you have written, you will understand what I meant when I said that you are nothing but unconnected, illogical, independent, un-clutched thoughts. For example, if you see a dog on the street, you will immediately remember the dog that made you afraid when you were young or one that you used to play with when you were young. The next thought would be about your childhood; the third, the teacher and the room you used to sit in school, and fourth, the place where your teacher used to stay.

You can see the thoughts flowing. There is no logical connection between the dog that you saw on the street and the teacher who taught you in school. But in a few seconds, you would have just drifted in that direction. There is no logical connection between the two; but your thoughts are moving, drifting from one thing to another.

Pain Shaft or Joy Shaft - Both Lead to Suffering

By your very nature you are unconnected, independent, illogical thoughts. Many things are happening within you. For the sake of your convenience, you pick up a few thoughts randomly, clutch them, create a shaft, and start believing that the shaft is you. You also believe that it is an accurate representation of your past and that it is your identity.

It is like when there are ten thousand flowers in different colors, you pick just a few flowers randomly and create a garland. You start thinking that the garland is the representation of the ten thousand flowers. The garland cannot be a representation of the ten thousand flowers.

Mostly, you create the shaft that your life is painful. Sometimes by mistake you even create a shaft with the idea that your life is joyful, but this is very rare and usually happens by mistake! Whatever shaft you create, whether it be 'life is pain' or 'life is joy', that shaft is not the representation of your past. It is not the totality of you.

Understand, you pick up thoughts in a very random way and connect them, clutch them and create a shaft.

Let me give you a diagram to help you understand how you clutch and create the shaft. It is a simple diagram to understand how thoughts flow in your being and how you connect them.

Each thought is a square or rectangle, different shape and different size. Thoughts are flowing in you, moving. One may be related to pain or a painful experience. Another one may be related to joy or a joyful experience. The next one maybe related to joy but you think of it as pain. It is referred to as JP (joyful experience, painful impression) on the chart. Similarly you may have a thought that is related to a painful experience but you may think of it as joy. We will refer to this as PJ (painful experience, joyful impression). Many times you may label pain as joy and joy as pain. Something continuously goes on in you. This is how

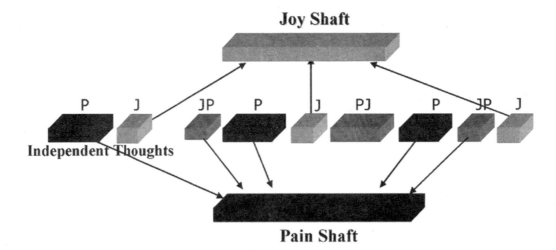

thoughts are flowing in you. Understand they are all completely unconnected, independent and illogical.

Each thought may be related to some experience which you had in the past or which you want to have in the future. All your thoughts are related to something about the past or something about the future. You cannot have thoughts about the present. In the present moment you can have only consciousness, not thoughts. The thoughts are either related to some joyful experiences which you had in the past and want to have in the future, or painful experiences which you had in the past which you don't want to have again.

Of course, sometimes you want to have pain because it boosts your ego. It satisfies your ego quite a bit. You can tell others, 'See how much I have struggled, how much I have suffered for you.' This is what you tell your children to create guilt in them, so that they listen to you.

Sometimes we go through suffering or we invite suffering because it gives us ego satisfaction. It can give us an identity and a feeling of fulfillment. This is why we allow suffering to happen. Many times we have vested interest in our suffering.

Sometimes, when you suffer you get attention from others. A small sickness like headache, fever, body pain are sometimes ailments which are nothing but ways to get the family's attention. The mind knows that with a little sickness, the whole family will you give attention; at a minimum they will listen to you. Nowadays, who listens to others? No one has time for that. So at least through ailments, we can get attention!

Actually, if you look inside yourself a little bit, you will understand that you create these small diseases just to get attention or to avoid tasks that you do not want to do. If you are asked or forced to do something that you don't want to do, you just say, 'I have knee pain,' 'I have this pain,' and 'I have that pain.' Once or twice you will say that as an excuse, and the third time you will see that really happening. Your mind is very powerful to create whatever you want. So beware.

Anyhow, some thoughts are related to some joyful experiences that you had in the past or that you want to have in the future. Some thoughts are related to pains that you previously had or which you don't want to have again.

There are so many thoughts, so many experiences moving like a conveyor belt inside your inner space, your inner consciousness. Some are related to joy and some are related to pain; some are related to the past and some to the future. Thoughts are constantly happening.

Each thought is completely independent, completely unconnected to the other thought. Understand, this is one of the important steps. No thought is logically connected. No thought holds responsibility for the other thought. They are all randomly appearing, independently appearing, illogically happening.

For archival purposes, you collect all the painful thoughts and create an idea that your life was depressing, that your life was pain, and you create a pain shaft. The moment you create a pain shaft, your life becomes hell. After the pain shaft is created, you will only pick up the painful incidents to confirm again and again what you believed in the first place.

They are all independent pain experiences, in no way connected to each other. But in your memory, you want to keep them all in one file for archival purpose, for reference. You put all your depression experiences in one file so that you can refer to that archive file.

Storing them all in one file for archival purposes alone is acceptable, but by and by you start believing that they are all connected to each other. This is where the problems start. Please understand that you do not evaluate arguments for the purpose of developing judgments. You develop opinions and subsequently collect only those arguments that support your pre-existing opinions. You have made ready the judgments in your life and you just collect arguments to support them.

So if you have already decided and are attached to the opinion that your life is painful, depressing, and full of suffering, then you will be just waiting to get more and more arguments to strengthen the judgments which you have already made about your life.

Rarely, you may create a joy shaft connecting all the joyful thoughts. You may start believing life is joy. Even if you do create a shaft that life is joy, you will also create the idea that there is an object which gives you joy, which is the reason for your joy. You will try to hang on to that object or person or incident or space. You may identify your joy with an object which may also be a person, place or an incident. Now you will try repeatedly to bring that object back in your life.

Any object that you are able to bring into your life again and again will not give you the same excitement as it gave you the first time.

The first time that you enjoy a sweet, the excitement is totally different. The first experience of the sweet is totally different from all the subsequent times you eat the sweet. It is the same with a person also. The first time that you meet, the experience is totally different; the excitement is totally different. In future meetings, the excitement will not be the same; the experience will not be the same.

That is why we say 'honeymoons' and not 'honeysuns'. Have you heard of the term 'honeysun'? No! What is the life of a moon? Sixteen days. A honeymoon is the excitement that will last for only sixteen days!

When you try to bring the same person, the same object, the same place again and again into your life, suddenly you will realize that the same excitement is not there. Please understand, the same person, the same object, the same place cannot bring the same excitement again and again. So whether you have created a pain shaft or a joy shaft, eitherway you have created hell for yourself.

Bliss is Choiceless

By connecting our thoughts in a linear way, we create the thought, 'I have pain,' 'I have suffering,' 'I have this,' 'I have that,' 'I am this type of person,' 'I am this type of being.' If we are blissful or joyful, we will try to extend this idea. We will try to stay in the same mood for some more time. If the idea is painful, we will try to break it. Neither

breaking nor extending is possible because the shaft does not exist in reality.

After a discourse, one of the devotees came up to me and said, 'Master, it is such a blissful experience for me. I am so clear about everything, I am afraid that I may lose this. Please tell me, how I can retain this.'

I told him, 'Do not try to retain the feeling. You felt the bliss because you understood that nothing could be retained. You felt the deep joy because you were choiceless. You felt the deep joy because you felt completely disconnected. You felt such a big relief because by your very nature you are un-clutched. The bliss was not because of the discourse itself. The discourse was a tool that made you experience your inherent un-clutched state, that's all. So now don't try to clutch again!'

If somebody comes and tells you, 'I am in ecstasy because I played tennis and I enjoyed it,' you think, 'Playing tennis brings ecstasy.' You create an equation. Now continuously you will be hitting the ball, playing tennis. But nothing will be happening in you, no ecstasy. Then you will think that the person who shared their tennis experience cheated you. Be very clear, he was not concerned about joy; he was completely relaxed while he was playing. Because of this, joy simply happened. But somehow he associated it with tennis, that's all.

Choicelessness is bliss. If you choose it, bliss will not happen because you have made a choice and thereby have eliminated it as a possibility.

When you are choiceless, when you are completely relaxed, bliss simply happens in you. When you are concerned about bliss, your very concern will ensure that you will not experience it.

Someone who is playing just hoping to achieve joy can play his best, but nothing will happen because you cannot do anything directly to get joy. When you decide that a certain person, object, or place may bring joy to your life and if you try to reproduce the feeling, you will see very clearly it will not bring the same experience of joy.

Knowing that the same object will not bring the same level of excitement in your life, but not being able to give up the hope or the pursuit of this excitement is 'addiction.'

You know that it is not and will not give you the same experience but you are not able to give it up. It is because you think that you have at least some excitement now and if you give this up, you are afraid what might happen. You are afraid you will be alone, and what you might do. That is what I call addiction.

Whether you create pain shaft or joy shaft, you end up in hell. Creating shafts will result in hell. If you create pain shaft then you will be creating pain. If you create joy shaft then you will be creating addictions. All addictions lead to hell. Whether you create a pain shaft or joy shaft, you are creating hell for yourself.

Understand that they are all independent experiences and in no way connected to each other.

The moment you try to retain an un-clutched experience, you clutch yourself. The clutching starts. The moment you clutch yourself, you create a shaft. Then you will be fighting to extend the shaft or destroy the shaft.

The moment you start trying to extend the shaft, you will start suffering because you will not be able to extend it. The moment you try to break the shaft, you will suffer because you will not able to break the shaft. Either way you will be a complete failure.

Understand only one thing - there is no shaft. Do not try to renounce your depression, because by your very nature it will be flowing, it will be going away. By your very nature just as joy disappears from your mind, depression also disappears from your mind. The moment you try to eliminate the depression, you will extend it and give it more life.

The Gap Between Thoughts - The Peace, The Bliss

Thoughts are purely independent just like water bubbles coming from the bottom of a fish tank. Just as independent water bubbles come up in a fish tank, independent thoughts come up in us. When the gap between them is too small, we think all the bubbles are connected to each other. But they are not connected. Each bubble is an individual, unconnected, illogical, independent, and un-clutched bubble. It is because the gap is so small that you think all the bubbles are connected.

It is the same way in our minds. By our very nature every thought is independent, illogical, unconnected and un-clutched. As with the bubbles, we experience a neutral space in between two thoughts. As the gap or the neutral space between the two thoughts is too small, we think all the thoughts are connected and that it is in the form of a shaft, but it is not.

When we change gears while driving a car, whether we change from neutral to first gear, first to second or second to third - whatever gears we may change, every time we have to pass through the neutral state. Only then we can go to the next gear, is it not? In the same way, we experience a neutral space in between any two thoughts. That neutral space, that silence is what I call peace, bliss. The peace that exists in us in between two thoughts is bliss. The gap between the thoughts, that neutral space is peace. This is bliss.

Unclutch - Work Smart, Not Hard

When you understand that you are unconnected, independent, illogical and un-clutched by your very nature, you will start experiencing the neutral space in you. With the knowledge of this neutral space in you, you will start living from moment to moment with spontaneity.

The moment that I utter the words that there is no linear connection between thoughts, people are completely shaken and frightened. Their first fear is, 'If that is the case, if I start living without connecting my thoughts, who will pay my bills? I may lose all my wealth, I may not remember where I kept all my money. I may not live in the society successfully.' Then you may start asking, 'How will I do my job? How will I take care of my things? Will I not just lie down in my bed without doing anything?'

The moment I say these things, the first question people ask, 'If I am un-clutched, why should I go to my office?' I ask, 'Why should you not go to your office?' The moment you ask that, it means that you have a little hatred or a little vengeance against the job. This is why the moment you find some excuse you want to escape from your work. You are expressing your anger, your violence against your routine, nothing else.

I always tell people, 'Alright, if you don't do anything and just be un-clutched, how many days will you be lying in your bed? Probably ten days at the most, until your *tamas*, your lethargy gets exhausted.' You have a certain amount of *tamas* in you. In Sanskrit, keeping quiet is *tamas*, doing hard work or restlessness is *rajas*, and doing smart work is *sattva* or pure intelligence.

Be very clear, if you just un-clutch, you will not work hard, you will work smart. Until your *tamas* gets exhausted you will lie there. But after that what will you do? Naturally you will start working; you will start moving! Do not be afraid that if you become un-clutched, you will not be able to do your daily routine.

I tell you, *what you think of as you* is not necessary to run your day-to-day life. This is the basic truth. This truth hurts us. If somebody is happy, independent of us, we can't tolerate it; it is too much. We want to feel that we are needed. That is why we project our suffering to the outer world. It makes us feel important.

You know that in your profession, the first thing you have to do is to convince your boss that the workload that you have is too much for any one person to handle. Second, if it can be done by one person, it can be done only by you. Third, it can only be done if you give your whole life to it. Only when you are able to convince your boss or your client of these three things, will you get a high compensation.

First, anybody who wants to exploit you has to instill a thought in you that you cannot live without him. Even your employee can exploit you if he can manage to instill a thought in you that without him your business cannot run. If he instills that thought in you, he can easily take advantage of you including cheating you.

In the same way your mind and your ego have created a churning thought, a fear in you that you cannot live, you cannot survive in a balanced way without it. The moment you accept this fear, the game is over. Your mind will completely exploit you. Your ego will completely cheat you. Please be very clear that all these things are only fears.

See, in the story of the blind man, he is not able to understand that he can walk without the stick after he gets his eyesight. Only when the man opens his eyes, only when he gets his eyesight, will he understand that he can walk without the stick. In the same way, only when you relax and understand that by your very nature you are unattached, suddenly you will realize you can live without a mind.

The walking stick is just an extra tool for the blind man. In the same way, the mind is an extra tool for you because by your very nature you don't need the mind to live. Because you have gone to such an extreme of relying on your mind, you cannot understand that you can live without the mind. You are afraid that you might go to the other extreme of being a mindless person with no morality in your life.

But let me tell you, a person who understands that by his very nature he is unattached, can never go beyond basic morality. It is only in his life that you will see a strong, deep sense of morality and it is only in his life you will see an extraordinary discipline. It will be a discipline which can never be shaken and a morality which can never be taken away. It will be morality which does not come out of fear or greed. Only in him, morality happens out of understanding. In all other beings, it happens out of fear or greed.

Morality based on fear or greed cannot take you beyond the body; it will constantly bind you to the body. Only when you understand that by your very nature you are unattached, a new beautiful morality starts happening in you and you start tasting and experiencing your being.

There are so many fears constantly happening within you. You might wonder that if you start living like this with no linear connection between one thought and another thought, how you can live your life. Do not get stuck with hypothetical questions. Just drop the mind and start living. You will see that you are able to do so quite effectively.

A small story:

> There was a Zen Master who was crossing a river with his disciple. Suddenly the disciple slipped and fell into the water and started shouting to his Master for help. He thought he was drowning. The Master just looked at him and said, *'Atma deepo bhava'* - Save yourself, guide yourself.
>
> The disciple cried out, 'Master, do not talk philosophy now! I am dying. Please help me!'
>
> The Master just said, 'Stand up,' ignored him and walked on. This was too much for the disciple to handle. He shouted out, 'Please help me, I am drowning.'

The Master simply turned around and shouted, 'Fool, I said stand up.' The disciple was completely shaken by the very voice of his master and he just stood up. To his surprise he found that the water came only up to the level of his waist!

You are always asking for help because you think you are drowning. Just stand up, the water is only up to your waist.

In this *sutra* Ashtavakra says, '*Virtue and vice, pleasure and pain are of the mind, not of you.*' They belong just to the shaft that does not really exist. They are not from your being. Only an enlightened master can boldly declare, *you are ever free.* Only he can say, *there is no virtue and vice, there is no pleasure and pain.* It is the people who want to keep you under their control who will never declare truths such as these to you.

Inducing Inferiority Complex - A Means to Exploit You

In almost all the fields, a person who wants to keep you in the position of a slave constantly tells you that you are weak in some way. People who want to keep you under their control socially will consistently beat into you the idea that you are weak.

In the film industry, where so much importance is given to appearance, a person who wants to keep you under his control will give you an impression that you are ugly. They project the movie stars in an extraordinarily beautiful way to make you feel that you are not beautiful enough. You would also find that it is normally the cosmetic industry that conduct the beauty contests to promote the idea of beauty which makes you believe that you are not enough unto yourself. You will not opt for cosmetics unless you feel that you are not enough unto yourself.

There is no need to constantly compare your body with some other body. God is not an engineer; He is an artist. If He were an engineer, then He would have made a mould and placed an order for one million Ms. Universe models and one million Mr. Universe models to be made and sent to Earth! But He is an artist who paints each one of us and carves each one of us. That is why each one of us is unique.

The very moment the thought enters your head that someone is more beautiful or more handsome than you, that very moment you create a gap between you and your body.

We can see in our own lives that many of us would like to look like someone else. The more you try, the more you feel that you are not looking like them. The moment you crave to look like someone else, a gap is created between you and your body. Then you start using cosmetic products and start trying all artificial methods to project yourself in a different way than you are. Unless you are given the idea that you are not enough unto yourself, you will not buy these artificial things. You will not help the cosmetic industry sell their products. So those who want to exploit you and sell their products give you the idea that you are not enough unto yourself.

Those who want to enslave us socially, give us the idea that we are weak and that they are necessary to protect us. A person who wants to sell his products teaches you that you are not enough unto yourself by putting these kinds of ideas in your mind. We forget that we have been created by the Divine. We start chiseling ourselves to further develop God's work and give it a final touch. We are trying to touch up and improve on His work; but it cannot be developed any further. It is perfect as it is.

Even in the spiritual field, people who want to keep you under their hold, consistently instill the idea in you that you are not enough

and you need to perform various meditations, *mantras*, *pujas* etc. so that you will go back to them again and again. In all three areas — socially, physically and spiritually, people try to exploit you by putting the idea in you that you are not enough unto yourself.

Only an enlightened master like Ashtavakra can liberate us from all these bondages. He gives us the truth straightaway with incredible honesty because he does not have a vested interest in controlling us. Honestly, I have never found direct truths such as the ones in *Ashtavakra Gita*.

Even when Krishna gives his teachings in the *Bhagavad Gita*, it is because of an ulterior motive to convince Arjuna to fight. Actually the entire gist of the *Bhagavad Gita* is narrated in just the two verses in the beginning in the second chapter when Krishna begins to talk. But the entire *Gita* consists of seven hundred verses delivered by Krishna to Arjuna in order to explain the supreme truth. In one of the chapters, Arjuna declares that he is more confused at the end than he was before asking Krishna to talk. Krishna talks continuously in seventeen chapters until Arjuna becomes completely tired and frustrated and surrenders to Krishna.

Sometimes when you torture people with your talk, they go out and praise you to others, so that others can also experience the torture and suffering!

Let me tell you an experience that happened to me:

> When I was in San Jose, some devotees were trying to get me to go on a roller coaster ride. Even though I refused, somehow they convinced me to consider it. Actually, devotees convincing the master happens more easily than the the master convincing the devotees!
>
> I said that first I would go and watch the people getting off the ride. If they

seemed to be coming out with joyful expressions on their face, then I would try the roller coaster ride. When I watched, I could see that the moment the roller coaster stopped, these guys getting off were screaming, shouting and were full of joy. That convinced me and I agreed to go on the next ride.

The first thing that happened when the ride started was my turban went flying! The ride was a complete churning process, from side to side and up and down. Now I tell people, that a roller coaster ride is just like marriage. Anyone sitting inside wants to jump out and the ones standing outside watching are tempted to try it at least once.

They had secured me to the seat with a belt and I had no means of escape until the ride was over, just like the belt around one's neck in a marriage. In many parts of India, instead of a wedding ring, a necklace is given to the bride as a token of marriage. In both the cases, whether it is marriage or roller-coaster, the belt is secure and one cannot even jump out!

After a minute or two, the roller coaster stopped and I was also screaming and shouting. It was then that I understood that the people getting off were screaming and shouting not out of excitement about the ride but because of the relief that the ride had stopped and it was over!

When I came out, the other devotees standing by asked me, 'How was the ride, Master?' I said, 'It is really good! Go, go, don't miss the ride.' I thought, 'Why should I be the only one that suffers! Let these guys also go and have the same experience!'

In the same way, if you were tortured in a discourse, you may repeat to others, 'You

can't see another *swami* like this. He is so intelligent. Please come tomorrow and listen to his lectures.' You make every effort for others to experience the same torture that you experienced.

In the *Bhagavad Gita*, Arjuna is completely tortured. If somebody recites seven hundred verses continuously in front of you, what will happen? But Krishna goes on reciting one after the other, what is one to do? Finally Arjuna tells Krishna, 'I do not know anything; I have given up. Please do whatever you want to.'

Then finally Krishna recites the *sloka* about surrender:

sarva dharmaan parityajya maamekam sharanam vraja

aham tvaam sarva papebhyo mokshayishyami ma shuchaha

'Abandon all varieties of religion and just surrender unto Me. I shall deliver you from all sinful reaction. Do not fear.'

Now what else can Arjuna do? Naturally he has to surrender. It is actually a technique. It is a method to make the other person surrender. Krishna had to employ this technique to tire Arjuna's logic out and make his surrender to the truth.

But here Ashtavakra has no other ulterior motive. He has only one motive: Janaka has to experience the truth that he has experienced. He has no other reason to speak. All he wanted to do was to transmit the experience, just to share the experience which happened in him.

He is creating the technology through which Janaka can experience the same thing which happened in him. That is why I say that *Ashtavakra Gita* is pure, honest truth. There is nothing in *Ashtavakra Gita* that can be removed, that can be edited out.

When the Seer is Affected by the Scene, Bondage Starts

Ashtavakra is pure energy and pure truth. That is the reason he is so courageous to declare: *Verily you are ever free.*

He is not playing with words such as your *atman* is free, you have to do this or that, etc. He says:

Verily you are ever free
You are the one seer of all and really ever free.
Verily this alone is your bondage that you see the seer as other than such.

When the seer (the one who is looking) is affected by the scene, the bondage starts.

Please understand, when the seer is affected by the scene, the problem in the form of bondage starts.

Your very being is pure. But the moment you start associating yourself as one other than the seer, the problem starts. This is the only bondage which you have. There is no other bondage.

I was telling you in the last discourse, Enlightenment–Guaranteed, how the bird is afraid and tries to hold on to the stick, thinking that if he lets go of the stick, he may drop and die. He does not realize that if he lets go, he will only fly. In the same way let me tell you: let go, you will only fly. You will never drop and die.

In *Vedanta* they say, *srishti-drishti* and *drishti-srishti*. It is not that the world is there and you see it. No! *Because* you see, the world is there! You need to understand that. But the next question that you will immediately ask will be, 'How can you say that Master? I am not the only one who sees it. The person next to me also sees the same thing. So how can you say that the world exists only because of the fact that I am seeing it?' Be very clear, the world exists just because you are seeing it.

Even the modern day psychologists say that you see only what you want to see. Your mind records only two percent of what is happening around you. You do not see what is happening; you only see what you want to see. You choose the two percent and see what you want to see.

Drishti-srishti means that you project in the way that you want to, you connect in the way that you want to and you understand in the way you want to. You don't see things as they happen or hear things as they are said.

Many times people ask me questions starting with, 'Master, you said this' and misquote me. I tell them, never say, 'You said'; always say, 'I heard.' Please be very clear, in the gap of time the word travels from one place to the other, the meaning becomes totally different.

Understand, you hear only what you want to hear and not what is actually spoken. In the same way, you only see what you want to see; you do not see what is actually in front of you.

When the seer is affected by the scene, the scene can never reflect reality. When the seer is affected by the scene, reality can never be seen. That is what Ashtavakra emphasizes here. When you start seeing yourself as anyone other than the seer, you are affected.

Sutra:

You who have been bitten by the great black serpent of egoism 'I am the doer'
Drink the nectar of the faith, 'I am not the doer' and be happy.

I think Janaka missed. Janaka missed what Ashtavakra was saying. That is why, now Ashtavakra has to compromise. In this *sutra* Ashtavakra also gives a technique.

If You Have Understood the Truth, There is No Need to Practice

Be very clear, techniques are given only to fools who simply miss the truth. An intelligent man does not need techniques. When the truth is spoken, the intelligent man immediately captures it and understands it. It is only the person who misses it who will ask, 'Master, what you said is really a beautiful truth, but how do I practice it?' The moment you bring the words, the question, 'How do I practice?' you have missed the truth.

When you understand that fire can burn you, do you ask, 'Master, I understand that fire will burn, but teach me how not to put my hand again and again in the fire so that I do not get burnt?' No, you don't ask this question! The very intelligence that fire burns is enough for you to keep your hands away and you will never put your hands near the fire again. If you think, 'This is the truth, but I should know how to practice it,' be very clear that you have not understood the truth.

To tell you honestly, the whole gist of Bhagavad Gita is in the first two statements made by Krishna. The moment he starts speaking which doesn't happen until the second chapter, he says:

*klaibyam maa sma gamah paartha naitat twayy upapadyate
kshudram hrdaya daurbalyam tyaktvottishtha parantapa* (2.3)

'O son of Partha, do not yield to this degrading unmanliness. It does not become you. Give up such petty weakness of heart and arise, O chastiser of the enemy.'

Just two verses - the whole gist of Gita is conveyed, but Arjuna simply missed it. And because Arjuna missed, Krishna has to continuously confuse him. Krishna has to completely tire Arjuna. Unless Arjuna's mind is exhausted, he cannot be helped; nothing can be done. So the first thing that needed to be done was to get Arjuna tired.

Arjuna was an intellectual person. He had lived with Krishna for more than thirty years. If you have lived around a master for

a long time and have not become enlightened, you become a dangerous intellectual. Arjuna had lived around Krishna for a long time and he had not become enlightened. This was a problem.

When you are an insider, without being an 'in-sider' you will create trouble. Arjuna was an insider; he knew the 'behind the curtain scenes'. But he had not realized the consciousness of Krishna. So naturally, he could have become a cunning criminal and a dangerous intellectual.

Dangerous intellectuals miss the truth. There have always been dangerous intellectuals. With Jesus, Judas missed the truth. I think he had become a dangerous intellectual. With Ramakrishna, it was a man named Hriday, and with Ramana Maharshi there was another such person. There are always a few people who live around the Masters and miss the truth. When they miss the truth, they become dangerous intellectuals. Here Janaka missed the essence of the teachings. That is the reason now Ashtavakra has to give a technique.

Sutra:

You, who have been bitten by the great black serpent of the egoism, 'I am the doer'
Drink the nectar of the faith, 'I am not the doer' and be happy.

Ashtavakra gives the technique. He tells Janaka, 'You think that you are the doer. Now start thinking, I am not the doer.' Please understand, simply thinking that 'I am not the doer' or having faith that 'I am not the doer' will not liberate you directly. But it will create a tremendous pressure in you, that you will become completely frustrated and drop everything.

People always come and tell me, 'Master, I tried to start meditating but I am not able to. Please advise me what to do.'

Meditation techniques are given to you just to make you understand that you cannot meditate.

Let me be very clear, this is the case with any meditation technique. In the last two and a half years, more than one million people have taken my meditation techniques. But I am boldly declaring that all meditation techniques are given to you just to make you understand that you cannot do any meditation technique continuously.

I am making another bold statement and if you are offended, I apologize. But it is the truth.

No intelligent man can practice any technique for more than twenty-one days with inspiration. He can practice it with perspiration, but never with inspiration.

I say that because, by your very nature you are intelligent and by your very nature you understand the truth. Techniques are just to make you tired, just to wear down the mind.

Here Ashtavakra is telling Janaka, 'Remember that I am not the doer.' Be very clear, this technique by itself will not liberate you. It will just make you tired. You will understand that you are not able to remember this on an ongoing basis. The moment that you understand that you are not able to remember 'I am not the doer' all the time, you will be completely frustrated and will just drop the mind. The moment you drop the mind, the truth that you are not the doer will simply become reality!

My Story

Now I will tell you a few things about my enlightenment. On the first day of the Ashtavakra discourse series, someone asked me if I could talk about my enlightenment. I asked him, 'Do you want an honest answer or a social answer?' He replied, 'Honest answer'. I said, 'Then please wait till the third day of the discourse.'

This is because, unless you get the glimpse of the truth, you will not be able to understand that I have achieved the truth, I have achieved Realization. Unless you experience the

technology created by me, you can never understand that I have discovered the truth.

Another person asked me, 'Master, in those days there was only one incarnation during each age. But nowadays, how are there so many incarnations, so many gurus, and so many enlightened masters?'

Modern man has become so complicated. Working with modern man has become so difficult. We need millions of masters. It is because we never listen when the truth is being stated.

Never think that you are listening to me. As long as I speak the words which relate with your logic or go with your vested interests, you will listen. The moment I say something that goes against it, you close yourself to these words. If you are courageous enough, stand up and question me. If you are not so courageous and want to be socially polite, you do not allow the words to enter into your being.

Either you stop and question, or you do not allow the words to get inside your mind. Be very clear, you are not listening. That is why I told the person who asked about my enlightenment that I would talk about it on the last day.

Let me tell you a few things:

I left home when I was very young, when I was seventeen. I started going to various monasteries, ashrams and wandered from village to village. I tried so many techniques, so many different methods. Of course, the ego and determination that I had at that young age helped me accomplish what I achieved.

To tell you honestly, if I talk about those experiences now, people call it *tapas* (ascetic practices) and what not, but actually it was not *tapas*. I was just enjoying it all. They ask me, 'Master, how did you do such great things? You are great. You are a Mahatma.' I tell them, 'Actually I think you are the

Mahatma, to be living in the same house, with the same car, same routine, same husband or wife! I cannot imagine living in the same house for more than a few months!'

It was not *tapas* for me. It was just freedom and I enjoyed the freedom. Everyday I was in a new place. I was experimenting with all these truths. I was playing with all these techniques. I even stayed inside the Taj Mahal for seven days. I related well with the security people there and lived in their quarters itself. Can you imagine this kind of freedom in your life?

After a few years of all this, the effortless withering away of the will was just happening in me. I had tried all possible techniques and methods. After seven or eight years suddenly one day, I was overcome by a deep depression. I started looking at my life from day one. I thought, 'What is happening? I have given my whole life for one objective and after all that, I have not experienced it. The cream of life is youth. I gambled with my youth. I have gambled my whole life for this idea of enlightenment.'

It is very easy to go to lectures and listen to all these concepts and go back to the same house, to the same spouse and live the same life. There is no need to take any risk. But I had gambled with my whole life.

Meditators are the ultimate gamblers. Ordinary people gamble with a little bit of money, a little bit of wealth. But meditators gamble with their whole life. I had sacrificed my whole life. The cream of my life had been sacrificed in this journey. Neither had I achieved the truth nor did I feel I was getting close to it. I was not able to convince myself that I was doing well. I was in deep depression.

You know what type of thoughts come when one becomes deeply depressed. I started thinking that the very idea of enlightenment was foolishness and it was just a conspiracy against humanity. I felt that a few egoistic people who wanted to claim that they were in some way higher, because they could not claim their superiority in any other field, had just started creating some concepts and had created this idea about enlightenment.

Honestly, that is what I thought. I thought that these people who had created this concept were the ones who were not able to create wealth and show that they were superior in any field. Neither had they achieved something in the political field to show their worth or success in the society, nor did they have good looks to go into some sort of show business! I thought that these were the people who could not achieve success in any field. Hence they created their own field, selling imagination, and created a new market!

My whole life was inspired by Ramakrishna. I had a beautiful photo of him, which I always carried with me. I used to offer *puja* (prayer) to this photo every morning. I used to constantly repeat a *mantra* twenty-four hours a day. I had mastered the technique of rolling the *japa-mala* (rosary) even in my sleep. Actually, it is not a big deal. Just try to sit and do *japa* (repeating the name of God); automatically you will learn the technique!

I had two *malas* with 108 beads in each one. I would hold one in each hand and if I finished chanting the *mantra* 108 times on one *mala,* I would move one bead on the second *mala*. By the time the 108 beads were completed on the second *mala*, I would have chanted the *mantra* 10,000 times. This is the way I practiced daily.

Once the frustration happened, it was so deep that I just picked up the photograph and threw it with full force. I also took both the *malas* that I was using for the repetition of the *mantra* and threw them into the Narmada river (sacred river in central India). Not only did I throw the *mala*, I said to myself, 'Along with these *malas*, I am throwing the *mantra* also; let it leave me.' I just threw the *mantra* along with the *mala*.

And let me tell you this: although it will be difficult for you to believe, this is honestly and exactly what happened. From that day, I forgot the *mantra* that I had been chanting for so many years. I simply forgot the *mantra*! It just left my mind completely.

I decided, 'Now I am neither going to do any further spiritual practice nor am I going to lead a life of *sannyas* (ascetic).' I decided to live as I wanted. First, I wanted to rest. Then, I thought I would get married or live a life as I wanted to, or live life as it comes. But I decided no more spiritual practice for me. I was convinced that the whole thing was a conspiracy against humanity. So I threw away the goal, the lifestyle, the practices, the *mala*, and the photos, and I rested.

Something happened in me. Because of the deep relaxation, suddenly something broke inside me. The un-clutching happened and the shaft never again became clutched!

Now, I know the view from both the sides, the view from that side and the view from this side. I know the struggles of that side, and I know the other shore also. That is why I tell you very clearly that no technique led me to the truth. Practicing different techniques only did one thing to me. It just made me tired and completely frustrated.

If some of you are frustrated, be very clear, blessed are those who are frustrated by

meditating. You have achieved the results of meditation. If you are frustrated by meditating you have achieved the desired result. It is time to drop the meditation, so drop the meditation.

People ask me, 'Master, you became enlightened because of your long *tapas*. How can I achieve enlightenment? How can that happen in us?' People ask me this again and again.

Let me tell you very clearly, I did a lot of *tapas* because I was just foolish. Be very clear, there is no need for any of these techniques or *tapas* to become enlightened. I can tell you how you should live to accomplish your goal of enlightenment because I lived in a manner that was not necessary. Because I lived the life which is not necessary, I can tell you what is necessary for you.

I had 10,000 keys in front of me and only one lock. The opening itself took only one second. Finding out the right key to open the lock took nine years. The time I spent playing with the keys is what you call as *tapas*.

I was playing and playing with 10,000 keys. The opening itself took only one second. Why should you play with 10,000 keys? Here I am giving you one key; straightaway open with it.

But you will say, 'When you played with 10,000 keys, why not us too?' Then go ahead and play; what can be done? Have the whole bunch and play. If you are really interested in getting liberated, there is no need to play with all the 10,000 keys.

But if you are interested in postponing the experience, like these professional seekers who claim to be seeking and studying for the last 30 years, then you are free to do so. These are the kind of people who come up to compliment me after my discourse, saying that I spoke very well. They will not be listening to me when I speak because they are busy creating words in their heads about how to come and compliment me after the discourse. Somehow they want to get attention and this is one way for them to do so, that is all. There is no need to compliment me.

Just digest the truth that is expressed. If it can enter your very being, then I will be content that whatever has to happen has happened.

When A Disciple Opens Up, the Master Also Happens

A master also grows with the disciple. To tell you the truth, as the disciple grows, the master also grows. That is why, in the Vedic system we say:

*Om sahanaa vavatu sahanau bhunaktu
sahaveeryam karavavahai tejas vina vadhee
tamastu maa vidhwishavahai
Om shanti shanti shantihi*

The Vedic prayer does not start as, 'May you be liberated.' Instead, it says, 'Let both of us grow.' Understand this one simple thing: a woman is a woman until she gives birth to a child. It is only after that she becomes a mother. When she gives birth, not only is the child given birth, the mother also goes through the birth of motherhood. Only after that she can be called a mother. Until then, she is just a woman. It is only at the time of the birth of her child, both baby and mother are delivered; the baby and the mother are born.

In the same way, when a disciple opens up, the master also happens. The disciple teaches the master and the master learns from the disciple. The master also grows with the disciple. If he can't grow or update himself, then he can never be a master.

Spiritual Freedom - The Base of the Vedic Tradition

Be very clear, enlightenment is not the end. It is the ultimate experience but not the final experience.

You need to understand these two words; they are very different. For example, let me tell you this: after the first day of discourse in this series, one person came to me and said, 'You have said everything. Why do we need one more class?' Yesterday another person said, 'Master, on the first day, I thought you could not take us much deeper; it is over. And today, suddenly I felt that you have taken us deeper than yesterday and you cannot take us any deeper than this. Everyday I feel that you cannot take us much deeper than this, but we do keep going deeper.' Everyday he felt that his experience was the ultimate.

Ultimate means living every moment totally, completely. Ultimate is not final, it can be updated.

Any enlightened master who cannot update himself can never be considered an enlightened master. Vedic masters are courageous to declare that even masters should update.

Krishna is courageous and bold to declare, *sambhavaami yuge yuge* - again and again I will come down. He is courageous to create space for the next generation of masters. He is not only concerned about the business of His time. Krishna understands that humanity needs spiritual masters at all times.

Any one can stand up and boldly express the wisdom of Krishna and anyone who expresses the wisdom of Krishna is Krishna. Krishna creates the space for other masters to come. This is the greatness of Krishna.

This is also the greatness of the Vedic *rishis*. They are not interested only in their own business. They are not egoistic that only their photos or only their influence should be there. They are ready to allow the next generation to update their work. Growth is possible only when you update.

Vivekananda beautifully says that freedom is the basic condition for any growth. I am questioned again and again in the West as to why we have so many Gods in India. I respond that it is because we had spirituality in the Indian cultural system. That is why we went to the heights and depths of spirituality.

The West has experienced social freedom for some time. As a result, they can change everything in their lives such as car, house and wife as frequently as they wish. They can constantly change things because of the social freedom.

In the Vedic system, at the age of seven, the child is given the Gayatri *mantra* (Vedic prayer to illuminate the intellect) that says, 'Let me meditate on the light that creates intelligence in me; let that intelligence help me meditate on it'.

Aum bhuh bhuvah svah tat savitur varenyam
Bhargo devasya dheemahi dhiyo yonah prachodayat

Only the torch is given. You have to start your journey with that.

Let me give you an example. If someone comes to you when it is dark, and asks you for directions to cross a forest, you could say, 'When I crossed earlier today, I walked seven miles straight ahead until I reached the place where there was a big snake. I walked four miles further until I saw a lion. At that point, I took a left turn and proceeded to walk seven more miles until I reached a river and crossed it. I walked four miles further in the same direction and then reached the other side of the forest.' Could anyone cross the forest with these instructions?

The snake would have left the place long ago and the lion would have moved somewhere else by then. Instead of giving directions in this manner, simply give him the torch and he will cross the forest by himself.

The Vedic culture had tremendous spiritual freedom, which is why there were 33 crore (330 million) deities. I think the population of the Earth must have been 33 crores at that time! Each one could have a customized God

and the people had the spiritual freedom to seek fulfillment in their own way. That is the beauty of the Vedic culture.

For any growth, freedom is the basic condition. Here, all techniques are created and given to you to make you understand that techniques cannot help. Instead, you need to go straight to the understanding.

If you are already tired of techniques, now is the time to drop your mind and look into yourself. Just understand this one truth, that by your very nature you are un-clutched. Again and again because of your social conditioning, fears and worries, you are trying to clutch yourself and make a shaft. Neither the shaft exists, nor does the continuity. You are just un-clutched. By your very nature you are un-clutched. The person who understands this does not need any technique. If you cannot understand, then you are free to torture yourself with the technique of constantly trying to remember, 'I am not the doer'.

Sutra:

Burn down the wilderness of ignorance with the fire of the knowledge,
I am the one and pure intelligence
And be free from grief and be happy.

Again, Ashtavakra comes up with one more technique. I think, when Ashtavakra spoke to Janaka saying, *'You are unattached by your nature'*, he did not see the light in Janaka.

This inner healing had not happened in Janaka at that point in time. That is why Ashtavakra had to compromise and create more techniques.

Burn down the wilderness of ignorance with the fire of the knowledge,
I am the one and pure intelligence
And be free from grief and be happy.

'I am the one and pure intelligence' -be very clear, the moment you start saying this, these words will start creating more and more

words in you. It is one of the beautiful techniques to completely tire you.

Instead, if you can straightaway understand and penetrate the truth with intelligence, you will see that by your very nature you are un-clutched. It does miracles in your being, in the physical level, mental level and in the being level.

When you understand the truth that by your very nature you are un-clutched, a tremendous, quantum transformation happens; transformation happens in a quantum manner, not in a step-by-step fashion. With just one leap, you can take a quantum jump and experience the truth, the awakening in yourself.

Our Mind Creates Our Body

All your physical and mental problems can be addressed by this single idea that you are un-clutched. The moment you understand that by your very nature you are un-clutched, that very moment your depression will simply disappear. The very idea of depression is created by you by constantly linking all your moods.

People ask me, '*Swamiji*, it is clear to me that the moment I understand that I am un-clutched by my very nature, depression will disappear. But how can physical healing happen?'

Be very clear, your body is directly guided by your mind. Let me explain two important things so that you can understand how the un-clutching brings better health or the healing effect in our body.

First, it is not only Yoga but medical science also that says that our body constantly rejuvenates; it also replaces itself. Please understand, it not only rejuvenates but it also replaces itself. We are constantly replacing ourselves. This is the first truth.

The second truth is an important truth that is again proven not only by yoga, but also by

biology and medical science - our mind creates our body. Five thousand years ago Yoga and Ayurveda sincerely started believing and experiencing that our mind creates our body. In this modern day, many scientific studies are proving that our mind creates our body. Our body is directly guided by our mind.

There is a book called 'Biology of Belief' written by Dr. Bruce Lipton. After 30 years of research in the field of biology, he came up with a powerful research report, in which he clearly proves that our positive and negative emotions play a major role in our body. They control our body in a bigger way than DNA and cells. Our body is guided by our beliefs, faith as well as positive and negative emotions. He says that even our body structure can be altered by our mind.

Step by step, he proves very clearly that all our genetic problems and all our physical and mental problems are created by our faith alone. He conducted several research studies, including some with children who had been separated from the biological parents from birth. The children would grow up thinking that the parents who had adopted them were their real parents. In these cases, the children even expressed all the symptoms of the diseases thought to be hereditary. He has done several studies similar to this. He has come up with a clear report that the body is directly guided by our faith, our beliefs as well as positive and negative emotions.

Biology repeatedly says that once in every 6 months, we create completely new body parts. Once a year not even a single cell of our liver is the same; the liver is completely replaced. And once in twenty-one days, our intestine is completely replaced. The skin gets renewed every five weeks and the skeleton is entirely new every three months. There is a specific number of days for each part of the body to get renewed.

Our body gets continuously updated. Our body has enough intelligence to replace itself. Our body is constantly replacing itself.

You may ask, 'Then why am I creating the same disease again in my body? If my body is again and again replacing itself, rejuvenating itself, then why are we carrying the same disease?' Because, you strongly believe in the same mind. Because you are carrying the same mind, you reproduce the same problems in the body. By clutching, by connecting, you stop the self-healing happening in your body.

The moment that you allow the inner healing to happen, the outer healing will simply start happening. The moment you understand that you are an un-clutched being, that moment the depression will disappear and I promise that you will create a completely new body. You will not carry your diseases forward to your new body.

It is because of your belief that you are connected and that you are a continuous flow, you carry the same disease. When you create the new part, you carry the same disease in the new part also. Just understand that you are completely un-clutched, you are disconnected and you are completely independent every moment.

Understand these two truths:

First, our mind creates our body and the second, our body is continuously replacing itself.

Now we can understand this statement: if we carry the same mind, the same shaft, we will reproduce the same disease or the same problem in the new body also. Everyday our body is creating a new body; it is automatically replacing itself. But because we carry the same mind, we bring the same disease back to our body and we force our body to suffer.

Let me tell you very clearly: based on my experience of having worked with at least 100,000 patients in two and a half years, who have come to me for healing or meditation, the moment you understand that you are an un-clutched being, you create a new body. You simply heal yourself. You come out of

not only mental problems, but even out of physical problems.

Be very clear, if we understand that we are un-clutched, if we realize the truth that we are un-clutched, unconnected, independent, illogical thoughts, we will stop carrying the same old identity and mind within us.

When we stop carrying the same mind and the same old identity, we will stop reproducing the same disease in the new body. We will stop reproducing the same pain, the same depression, the same difficulties and same disease in the new body.

If you are un-clutched, you will allow your body to heal from the disease which you already have and you will create a new body, a new system, which will be more immune, energetic and alive.

You are bringing the same diseases into the body by bringing the same old mind, by clutching yourselves with your past. You are not allowing the body to heal itself. You are not encouraging the body to rejuvenate and replace itself. The body by its very nature constantly replaces itself. You are stopping the healing process by clutching and connecting to your past.

For example, if your mother has conditioned you in your young age that if you play in the rain you will catch a cold, the memory gets engraved in you and even after thirty or forty years, you do not even have to go out when it rains - if you see the rain through the window, you will start sneezing. When you bring the old engrams, when you bring the past conditioning, when you bring the past and connect it with the present and make a shaft, you abuse the future.

Unclutching dramatically improves your health and brings a healing effect in you. Almost all the mental problems related to desires, guilt, fear, addiction, depression etc can be addressed with this single truth that you are unclutched.

All depressed moods are nothing but clutching all low moods and creating a shaft of depression. For example, the low mood that you suffered ten years ago, the low mood that you suffered nine years ago, the low mood that you suffered eight years ago, the low mood that you suffered seven years ago, the low mood that you suffered six years ago - they are all unconnected, independent, illogical experiences that happened in your life.

When you connect all of them, clutch and see them as a shaft, you say, 'Oh, my life was a depression.' The moment you start believing that you are a depressed being, you will create more and more arguments, collect more and more data to prove your judgments, to prove your understanding. Then naturally you will label yourself as a depressed being, 'I am depressed.'

Understand that all your mental problems, whether related to addiction, depression or low moods, everything is directly related to this clutching. If you understand this single truth, the ultimate technique that by your very nature you are un-clutched, suddenly you will see that so many mental problems disappear by themselves. You do not have to do anything; they will disappear by themselves.

When you understand you are un-clutched you can work on your physical aches and pains; they will be healed. For example, the knee pain you had ten days ago, the knee pain you experienced nine days ago, the knee pain you had eight days ago are all unconnected, independent experiences. But when you connect all of them and put a label, 'I have knee pain,' you make a shaft.

If you understand your un-clutched nature and stop creating shafts, you will see your pains dissolving. Pain becomes pain because you label it as pain. Depression is depression because you create a shaft of depression.

If you allow your mind to un-clutch from your past, you will create a new body without

old ailments. You will create a new body, which will be more balanced, more energetic, have more healing power and more immunity.

If you strongly believe that you had knee pain for ten years, naturally you will strongly believe you are going to have the same knee pain for the rest of your life. This faith is more than enough to reproduce and create a knee pain in the new body that you create every morning. Because you clutch with the same mind, connect with the same mind, you reproduce the same disease in the new body that you create everyday.

Unclutch and Get Rid of Your Guilt and Vengeance

When you un-clutch from your thoughts, from this shaft, you will suddenly see a new inner healing happening in you. You will forget about whomever you were not able to forgive. You will not just forgive, you will even forget about the whole thing.

I am not only talking about forgiving others. Many times the most difficult person to forgive is yourself. You might not be able to forgive yourself for the decisions that you have made, the life that you have led, the relationships which you have maintained or the actions that you have done in your life.

When you cannot forgive yourself, it is called guilt. When you cannot forgive others it is called vengeance. When you un-clutch, both guilt and vengeance will disappear. Not only will you forgive, you will also forget because there is no connection between your behavior and these thoughts.

The mistakes that you made ten years ago, the mistakes that you made eight years ago, the mistakes that you made seven years ago are independent, unconnected incidents that happened in your life.

When you connect all of them and think, 'I am the worst person because I have done all these things,' you do not realize the hell that you are creating for yourself.

A Quantum Jump - Free From the Past

You may ask, 'Then how can we learn from past experience, Master?' That is another important question. Be very clear, you will never be able to learn from past experiences. Past experience can only make you do the same things again and again. Any memory about the past experience can only make you do the same thing in a larger or smaller way, but the quality will be the same.

You will never be able to take a quantum jump by connecting, by clutching.

Be very clear, you will never be able to achieve any significant transformation or change in your personality by remembering your past.

All of you are trying your best to update yourself by remembering your past. Have you been successful? No! Because when the past is remembered, it has the power to make you repeat the same behavior again and again and again. You will be made to do the same mistakes again and again.

So be very clear, connecting with the past is in no way going to help you to update yourself, upgrade yourself, transform yourself. Whether you want physical health, mental well being or emotional balance, the basic thing that you need to do is un-clutch.

A connected, clutched mind creates more and more miseries in our personal life, professional career and relationships. It tremendously affects our creativity and economic wellbeing.

When we un-clutch, the first thing that will happen to us will be the inner healing effect - a deep silence and peace in us.

Second, that inner healing will start radiating in the physical wellbeing, which is our health.

Third, naturally it will start radiating in our relationships.

Fourth, because these three are going beautifully, we will be creative and productive.

Unconscious or Subconscious Mind - A Pure Myth

It may be a little difficult for you to digest these truths. People ask me, 'Master, the problem does not seem as simple as you make it appear; it is a deep-rooted unconscious problem.'

Please be very clear, I am making a bold, courageous and challenging statement. Of course, I have the support of the Vedic *rishis* who have dived deep into consciousness, who have done enough research in the inner world and consciousness.

Man does not have unconscious or subconscious mind as it is taught to us.

It is a very challenging and bold statement. It goes against the theory of psychoanalysis, all the theories of psychology and the modern philosophies, which try to explain the workings of the mind. Be very clear, the modern day psychologists have only worked with sick people. They have observed only sick specimens. Not one fulfilled being was a part of their research. So the standard which they set as normal is itself abnormal. Freud did not have an opportunity to work with a Buddha. Adler did not have an opportunity to have a Ramakrishna as a specimen.

So be very clear, the idea of unconscious or subconscious is one more concept to create more fear. One group of people has created the idea of sin and guilt and another group has created the idea of subconscious and unconscious, both of which exploit the masses.

Every master who has worked on the inner space, who is awakened, knows that you do not have unconscious or subconscious mind.

The idea of unconscious or subconscious is a concept that just creates more fear. The idea of sin and guilt and the idea of unconscious and subconscious are concepts that could exploit people.

The concept of sin and guilt has been created to always keep *you* down, to take your confidence away. If someone does not feel guilty, he cannot be exploited. So the moralistic ideas have been created, which could cause guilt in you so that you could be exploited on an ongoing basis.

Oh Sons of Immortality!

The one and only sin that you commit is clutching to the old thoughts and creating a shaft. Be very clear, you may commit an act which society labels as sin. But you are not a sinner.

This is why the Vedic *rishis* are beautifully addressing you as *amrutsya putraha* – Sons of Immortality! You are, by your very nature, immortal. There is no need to achieve that state separately.

*Shrunvantu vishve amritasya putraha
vedahametam purusham mahantam*

The *rishis* do not address you as sinners. They say, 'Oh, sons of immortality.' For practical purposes we have started translating the word *putra* as son. But the literal translation for the word *putra* is 'outcome'.

You are the outcome of the intense enlightened experience.

Again and again, the *rishis* declare this one truth: you are much more than the two identities which you carry.

If one says that you are a sinner, then you can conclude that they have a vested interest in you believing that you are a sinner. When you make all the people around you believe that they are lower level people, then you have the confidence that you are a higher person, you are somebody important or 'holier than

thou'. But the Vedic *rishis* are not speaking in that language. If they say, 'you are sinners', then you can say they are talking out of vested interest. But the *rishis* are saying that you are much more than your identity; they are saying that you are God.

Shrunvantu vishve amritasya putra
vedahametam purusham mahantam

Only a man who has experienced this truth, who has the courage to tell this truth to others, who trusts his disciples with the thought that, 'Even if I give him this courage and confidence, he will respect me, he will not disrespect me', only when you have that much courage, this truth can be reproduced.

The *rishis* were not only experienced, they had tremendous trust as well. They were only concerned about reproducing that solid experience. They did not give importance to anything else. They did not give importance to their name or their identities because they realized that they were much more than these two identities.

The person who realizes that he is much more than these two identities will never be shaken by the confusions, problems and dilemmas of these two identities. All your problems, including physical health - please understand when I say including your physical health, I mean all the diseases that you suffer in the body - are only because of these two identity problems.

You have neither a subconscious nor an unconscious mind. You have neither sin nor guilt. Be liberated from this sin and guilt, which is the *mamakar*, the identity that you carry in the inner world; and the unconscious and the subconscious which is the *ahankar*, the identity that you project to the outer world. Be liberated from these two from today. Both these identities are lies.

Look very clearly: you can have only one thought at a time, am I right? Is there any special being, anybody who is here, who can have two or three thoughts at a time? No, you cannot. You can have only one thought at a time. Then where is the question of subconscious or unconscious?

Afraid of Death - Just Have a Cup of Coffee!

Be very clear, we can have only one thought at a time and each thought replaces the thought that precedes it. Each thought that comes up replaces the thought that precedes it.

People come to me and ask me, 'My whole life is filled with the fear of death. I don't know what to do. How can I get rid of this fear?'

I tell them, 'Just have a glass of water or a cup of tea.'

They say, 'What is this *Swamiji*? How can a cup of tea or having a glass of water help me get out of my fear of death?'

I tell them, 'Come and sit, have a cup of coffee now.' When they are having coffee, I ask them, 'What happened to the fear of death?'

They say, 'For that moment, it was not there *Swamiji*.'

All you need to do is just have a cup of coffee!

The moment you have the thought that you want to have a cup of coffee, the thought of fearing death has been replaced. It has disappeared!

It is simple logic: the moment you decide to stand up, you renounce the thought of sitting. The moment you decide to walk out of a place, you renounce the thought of staying inside. The moment you decide to come in, you renounce the thought of standing outside. Every thought is replacing the earlier thought. At every moment you are renouncing your thoughts.

Understand, every moment you are renouncing your thoughts according to your very nature. The moment you decided to have a cup of coffee, you have already renounced the thought of fearing death. The fear of death is replaced by the thought of having a cup of coffee.

A big problem would be if you would say, 'Master, when the fear comes back, what is one to do?' Be very clear, the moment you decide that the fear will come back again, you are bringing back the fear. It is not coming back. Your strong faith that it will come back brings the fear back.

Why are you bringing it back again? It has already left you.

You will ask me, 'How can it be so simple?' You have always been taught and been made to believe that it is not so simple. It IS that simple. If you really understand this, it is so simple.

People are constantly telling me that it is not so easy. But I am telling you literally it is so easy. Nothing needs to be done. A simple understanding is all that is needed.

For example, guests do not come to your home unless you invite them. Not only do you invite them, you send them e-mails, written invitations, leave voice messages, and fax them. After that, you even send someone to personally pick them up and transport them to your home. Once they enter your house you say, 'Oh, I didn't think you would come.'

In the same way you send messages to your mind that produces the thought that you have a strong faith that the fear of death is going to come back. When you have a strong fear, when you have a strong idea, when you have a strong desire that the fear is going to come back, you fulfill your desire and the fear comes back.

Understand, every moment by your very nature, you are replacing your thoughts.

People ask me, 'Master, I am suffering with too many sexual thoughts. How can I escape from them? How can I get rid of them?'

I tell them, 'Sit here. For one hour, meditate on sex.'

After that they open their eyes and say, 'Master, the mind is not able to stay on the same subject; it is going everywhere!'

The person who came to me and said that he was consumed by these sexual thoughts was complaining that he was not able to get rid of them. When I told him to concentrate on that thought, he said he was not able to do so. What does that mean? By your very nature, you are unconnected, independent, illogical, unconnected thoughts.

You neither have to worry about your fears, nor do you have to worry about your greed.

Your worry about your worries, your worry about your fears, your worry about your greed is the only problem. Your fear is not the problem; your fear about the fears is the problem.

Similarly, you are not afraid of your failure. You are afraid of your fear of failure, not failure itself.

For example, you know for certain that by the end of this year, you are not going to be a billionaire. Are you worrying about it or are you suffering saying, 'I am not going to be a billionaire. What will happen to me?' No, you do not suffer because of that! But you will always suffer with the thought, 'Will I have one hundred thousand dollars or not?'

Suffering is because of that uncertainty.

Fear is because of the possibility of not achieving your goal. Fear is not connected to your failure. Fear is connected to your fear of failure.

If you are haunted by greed or fear, it is just because of your clutching and connecting.

If you understand this one truth, that constantly you renounce, constantly you replace your own thoughts, just a glass of water is enough to get rid of your fear of death! Because the moment you decide to have a glass of water, the thought of the fear will have already disappeared. If the thought of death was so strong, it would still be there. Instead it can easily be replaced by just a single cup of tea. A cup of tea is more than enough. A glass of water is more than enough to get rid of the fear of death, to get rid of great grief, to get rid of any problem in your life.

Whatever problem you may have, you can have only one thought at a time. Can you have two or three thoughts at a time? No. So be very clear that your enemy is only one thought. When you start believing in unconscious and subconscious, you make your enemy too powerful. You clutch all the thoughts. The problem is not a single thought of fear. The problem is that you connect all the thoughts of fear that you have had since your birth, create a shaft and start to believe, 'I am filled with fear.'

The fear of death which happened in you ten years ago, the fear of death which happened in you nine years ago, the fear of death which happened in you eight years ago, the fear of death which happened in you yesterday, are all unconnected, independent, illogical, un-clutched fears, un-clutched thoughts. When you connect all of them and create a shaft, you conclude, 'My life is filled with fear.' The moment that you create that shaft, you create hell for yourself. And you start suffering with it.

Be very clear, do not empower your enemy before fighting with him. What you are doing is empowering the enemy, your mind, and then trying to kill it.

First, you need to understand that you cannot kill him because he does not exist. If he exists, you can fight with him. But you are fighting with a shadow, you are fighting with darkness, you are fighting with someone who does not exist.

Mind is a myth. Your ideas about pain or pleasure are a pure myth. In Sanskrit we call it *maya*. *Maya* means *ya ma iti maya*. Literal translation of the word *maya* in Sanskrit is *that which does not exist, but which gives an experience as if it exists*.

Understand that your mind, your fear, your greed, do not exist. Just because you clutch all your thoughts and see, it gives you a feeling as if they do exist.

If you are un-clutched, you will understand the simple truth that the mind is a myth. Whatever you think of as you is a lie. When you stop connecting and creating a shaft, suddenly you open up to the truth that by your very nature you are an unconnected, illogical, un-clutched being.

I have only one message from Ashtavakra: **You are an un-clutched being**. By your very nature you are unattached. All you need is the courage to let go.

Be Liberated

We are like the bird that is holding on to the hunter's trap, afraid to let go without realizing that it can just fly and be liberated if only it would let go. In the same way, we are holding on to our mind and ego, which are nothing but non-existent shafts. We cling to things that do not even exist. We are bound by the mind which itself is a myth. The bird, which is trying to hold on thinks that if he lets go he may fall and die. If we let go we will only fly; we will never fall and die.

Similar to the bird trap, hunters have a trap to catch monkeys also. They catch monkeys using a small box for a trap. They place some sweets inside a box. The monkey puts its hand inside the box and grabs the sweet. As long as

the monkey is holding onto the sweet, it will not be able to take its hand out because its fist is larger than the hole. If the monkey lets go of the sweet, it could remove or slide its hand out immediately. But the monkey is not intelligent enough to realize that. It holds on to the sweet and just because it is holding it, it is not able to take the hand out. If it just lets go of the sweet, it can take its hand out and be free.

In the same way, the bird holds on to the stick because of its fear that it may fall and die. But even by hanging on to the stick, it is not going to live long. It just waits for the hunter to come and grab it. If it just lets go, it can simply fly.

You are also clutching on to the mind and the ego and waiting for Yama - the Lord of Death. If you just let go, you also can simply be free and fly.

If you imbibe and understand these truths, the enlightenment experience can be yours, you can simply have it. Liberate yourself!

May you radiate the eternal bliss, nithyananda.

APPENDIX

About Paramahamsa Nithyananda

Paramahamsa Nithyananda is a living enlightened Master of the 21st century.

He took birth in Tiruvannamalai, a spiritual nerve center in South India. Since a very young age, Nithyananda spent days and nights in meditation in the divine aura of Arunachala. His intense quest for deeper Truths of life led him on his spiritual journey which covered the length and breadth of India, several thousand miles of which he covered on foot. Visiting venerated shrines, meeting highly evolved *yogis* and *rishis*, and practicing intense meditations, he studied Yoga, Tantra, and other Eastern metaphysical sciences.

He went through several profoundly impacting spiritual experiences, culminating in his realization of the Ultimate at a young age.

Since then, Nithyananda has been sharing his experience with millions of people worldwide through the activities of Nithyananda Mission which conducts insightful and inspiring meditation programs and a wide spectrum of social services, thus providing life solutions at the physical, mental and spiritual levels. The meditation programs are offered worldwide through the International Vedic Hindu University (IVHU) Florida, USA. Further, free education to youth, encouragement to art and culture, corporate meditation programs, meditation for prisoners, free medical camps, free meals, a one-year residential training program in India called the Life Bliss Technology program, an in-house *gurukul* system of learning for children, and many more such services are offered around the world.

Employing time-tested *vedic* knowledge and modern technology, the Mission ashrams and centers the world over serve as spiritual laboratories where inner growth is a profound achievement. Today, they are much sought after as ideal destinations to explore, experiment and

experience through a host of programs, courses and research facilities in diverse subjects from meditation to the sciences.

Established in 2003, Nithyananda Mission has grown today into a worldwide movement for bliss, standing for the ideal of realizing an enlightened humanity and thereby raising the collective consciousness of planet earth.

Programs and Workshops

Nithyananda Mission offers specialized meditation programs worldwide, to benefit millions of people at the levels of body, mind and spirit. A few of them are listed below:

Life Bliss Program Level 1 (LBP Level 1)
- Energize yourself

A *chakra* based meditation program that relaxes and energizes the seven major *chakras* or subtle energy centers in your system. It gives clear intellectual and experiential understanding of your various emotions such as greed, fear, worry, attention-need, stress, jealousy, ego, and discontentment. It is designed to create a spiritual effect at the physical level. It is a guaranteed life solution to experience the reality of your own bliss. When you are liberated from a particular emotion, you experience a new world, a new energy. It is a highly effective workshop, experienced by millions of people around the globe.

Life Bliss Program Level 2 (LBP Level 2)
- Death demystified!

A meditation program that unleashes the art of living by demystifying the process of dying. This program creates the space to detach from ingrained and unconscious emotions like guilt, pleasure and pain, all of which stem from the ultimate fear of death. It is a gateway to a new life that is driven by natural intelligence and spontaneous enthusiasm.

Life Bliss Program Level 3 - Atma Spurana Program (LBP Level 3 - ATSP)
- Connect with your Self!

An indepth program that analyzes clearly the workings of the mind and shows you experientially how to be the master of the mind rather than be dictated by it. It imparts tremendous intellectual understanding coupled with powerful meditations to produce instant clarity and integration.

Life Bliss Program Level 3 - Bhakti Spurana Program (LBP Level 3 - BSP)
- Integrate your Devotion

A program that reveals the different dimensions of relating with others and with your deeper self. It clearly defines relationship as that which kindles and reveals your own unknown dimensions to you. It allows you to experience the real depth and joy of any relationship in your life.

Life Bliss Technology (LBT)
- A free residential life sciences program

Life Bliss Technology (LBT) is a residential program for youth between 18 and 30 years of age. With its roots in the Eastern system of *vedic* education, this program is designed to empower modern youth with good physical, mental and emotional health and practical life skills. By nurturing creative intelligence and spontaneity, and imparting life skills, it creates economically self-sufficient and spiritually fulfilled youth. Above all, it offers a lifetime opportunity to live and learn under the tutelage of an enlightened master.

Nithya Spiritual Healing
- Healing through Cosmic energy

A unique and powerful means of healing through the Cosmic energy, this is a meditation for the healer and a means to get healed for the recipient of the healing. Nithyananda continues to initiate thousands of Nithya Spiritual Healers worldwide into this scientific and time-tested healing technique which has healed millions of people of ailments ranging from migraine to cancer.

Inner Awakening

An enlightenment intensive program for sincere seekers offering yoga, powerful teachings, meditation, initiation and more. This program is an intense experience to prepare the body-mind system to hold and radiate the experience of 'living enlightenment'.

Nithyanandam

An advanced meditation program for seekers where the presence of the Master and the intense

energy field lead one to the state of *nithya ananda* – eternal bliss. It offers a range of techniques from meditation to service to sitting in the powerful presence of the master.

Kalpataru

An experiential meditation program sowing in one the seed of:

Shakti, the Energy to understand and change whatever you need to change in life,

Buddhi, the Intelligence to understand and accept whatever you don't need to change in life,

Yukti, the Clarity to understand and realize that however much you change, whatever you see as reality is itself a continuously changing dream,

Bhakti, the Devotion, the feeling of deep connection to That which is unchanging, eternal and Ultimate, and

Mukti, the Ultimate Liberation into Living Enlightenment when all these four are integrated.

Nithya Dhyaan
- Life Bliss Meditation

Become one among the millions who walk on planet Earth – Un-clutched! Register online and get initiated.

Nithya Dhyaan is a powerful everyday meditation prescribed by Nithyananda to humanity at large. It is a formula or a technique, which is holistic and complete. It works on the entire being to transform it and make it ready for the ultimate experience of enlightenment to dawn. Each segment of this technique complements the remaining segments to help raise the individual consciousness. It trains you to un-clutch from your mind and live a blissful life. It is the meditation for Eternal Bliss.

If you wish to be initiated into Nithya Dhyaan, you may visit http://www.dhyanapeetam.org and register online. You will receive through mail, a *mala*, bracelet, a spiritual name given by Nithyananda for your own spiritual growth (optional), Nithya Dhyaan Meditation CD and Nithya Dhyaan booklet in a language of your choice, personally signed by Nithyananda (mention your choice in the comment column).

Nithyananda says, 'My advent on planet Earth is to create a new cycle of individual consciousness causing Collective Consciousness to enter the Superconscious zone.'

Nithyananda Mission Highlights

- **Meditation and de-addiction camps worldwide:** Over 2 million people impacted to date
- **Nithya Spiritual Healing:** A system of cosmic energy healing administered free through 5000 ordained healers, through our worldwide ashrams and centers, touching 20,000 people globally every day – healing both mind and body
- *Anna Daan*: **free food program:** 10,000 nutritious meals distributed every week through all the ashram *anna mandirs* for visitors, devotees and disciples thus improving health standards
- **The Nithyananda Order and its training:** Spiritual aspirants ordained as *Sannyasis, Brahmacharis and Brahmacharinis*: who undergo years of intensive training in yoga, meditation, deep spiritual practice, Sanskrit, *vedic* chanting, life skills, and who run the 100% volunteer based ashrams of Nithyananda Mission worldwide, working in all Mission activities
- **International Vedic Hindu University (IVHU)** (the former Hindu University, Florida, USA): Paramahamsa Nithyananda was unanimously elected as chairman (chancellor) of International Vedic Hindu University which provides education in Eastern philosophies, therapeutics, *vedic* studies, meditation science and more through Bachelor of Science, Post Graduate and Diploma degrees
- **Nithya Yoga:** A revolutionary system of yoga in the lines of sage Patanjali's original teachings, taught worldwide.
- **Temples and Ashrams:** Over 30 Vedic temples and ashrams worldwide.
- **Meditation Programs in prisons:** Conducted in prisons and juvenile camps to reform extremist attitudes – resulting in amazing transformation among the inmates.
- **Medical Camps:** Free treatment and therapies in allopathy, homeopathy, ayurveda, acupuncture, eye check-ups, eye surgeries, artificial limb donation camps, gynecology and more

- **Support to children in rural areas**: School buildings, school uniforms and educational materials provided free to rural schools.
- **Life Bliss Technology**: A free two year / three month program for youth teaching Life Engineering and the science of enlightenment
- **Nithyananda Gurukul**: A modern scientific approach to education combined with the *vedic* system of learning – protecting and developing the innate intelligence of the child who flowers without repression, fear or peer pressure
- **Corporate Meditation Programs**: Specially designed and conducted in corporate firms worldwide including Microsoft, AT&T, Qualcomm, JP Morgan, Petrobras, Pepsi, Oracle, American Association of Physicians of Indian Origin (AAPI) – with focus on intuitive management, leadership skills and team work.
- **Nithyananda Institute of Teachers' Training**: Over 300 teachers trained to teach: transformational meditation programs, Quantum Memory Program, Nithya Yoga, Health and Healing Programs, Spiritual Practice Programs and more
- **Media**: Articles in national and international newspapers and magazines, carrying transforming messages from Nithyananda
- **Nithyananda Publishers**: Over 4700 hours of Paramahamsa Nithyananda's discourses transcribed, edited and published in-house and made available in stores through books, DVDs and CDs
- **Life Bliss Gallerias**: Worldwide stores and mobile shops retailing recordings and books of Nithyananda's discourses and Nithya Kirtan recordings in 23 languages
- **Nithyananda Meditation & Healing Centers**: Worldwide, offering meditation and healing services
- **Nithyananda Sangeeth Academy**: Music, dance and other forms of art taught and encouraged in youth and elderly alike - live and through internet
- **Free Discourses on YouTube**: Over 500 free discourses on www.youtube.com – wisdom from the Master, easily accessible. Ranked top in viewership

- **Support to scientists and researchers:** Continually bridging gaps between science and spirituality through researches on spiritual energy and healing.
- **Nithyananda Youth Foundation:** A collection of inspired youth, building a divine and dynamic society with a common ideology of peace and enlightenment
- **Nithya Dheera Seva Sena:** Through transformation of self, this volunteer force of *Ananda Sevaks* trains and functions in the service of humanity, also serving as relief wing working towards disaster recovery management.

Contact Us

Listed below are some of the main centers of Nithyananda Mission.

USA:
Los Angeles
Los Angeles Vedic Temple
9720 Central Avenue, Montclair, CA 91763
USA
Ph.: +1 909 625 1400
Email: programs@lifebliss.org
URL: www.lifebliss.org

MALAYSIA:
Kuala Lumpur
14, Jalan Desa Gombak 5, Taman Desa Gombak
53000 KL, MALAYSIA
Ph.: +601 78861644 / +601 22350567
Email: murthi.kasavan@gmail.com, manirantaraananda@gmail.com
URL: www.mynithyananda.com

INDIA:

Bengaluru, Karnataka
(Spiritual headquarters and Vedic Temple)
Nithyananda Dhyanapeetam, Nithyanandapuri,
Off Mysore Road,
Bidadi, Bengaluru - 562 109
Karnataka, INDIA
Ph.: +91 +80 27202801 / +91 92430 48957
Email: mail@nithyananda.org
URL:www.nithyananda.org

Varanasi, Uttar Pradesh
Nithyananda Dhyanapeetam
Leelaghar Bldg, Manikarnika ghat
Varanasi, INDIA
Ph.: +91 +99184 01718

Hyderabad, Andhra Pradesh
Sri Anandeshwari Temple, Nithyananda Giri,
Pashambanda Sathamrai Village, Shamshabad
Mandal
Rangareddy District - 501 218
Andhra Pradesh, INDIA
Ph.: +91 +84132 60044 / +91 98665 00350

Salem, Tamil Nadu
Nithyanandapuri, 102, Azhagapurampudur
(Behind Sharada College), Salem – 636 016
Tamilnadu, INDIA
Ph.: +91 +427 2449711

Tiruvannamalai, Tamil Nadu
Nithyanandapuri, Girivala path
Tiruvannamalai – 606 604
Tamilnadu, INDIA
Ph.: +91 +4175 237666

Rajapalayam, Tamilnadu
Nithyanandapuri, Kothainachiarpuram,
Sankaran Coil Road,
Rajapalayam, Virudhunagar District
Tamilnadu, INDIA
Ph.: +91 +4563 230001 / +91 +98421 30008

Pondicherry
Nithyanandapuri,
Embalam to Villianoor Main Road,
Embalam Post, Pondicherry - 605 106
INDIA
Ph.: +91 94420 36037 / + 91 97876 67604

For further information visit
www.nithyananda.org

Nithyananda Galleria

A wide range of products for blissful living:
- Nithyananda's insightful messages on video, audio tapes, CDs and books in over 20 languages.
- Enlivening music and chants for meditation and deep inner healing.
- Meditation and yoga books, kits and CDs for rejuvenating body, mind and spirit.
- Energized rosaries, bracelets, photographs, clothing and gift items for a stimulating life style.
- Ethnic energy bead jewelry for men and women for tranquility and continued high energy.

Visit www.lifeblissgalleria.com for more information.

Suggested for Further Reading

- Guaranteed Solutions
- Don't Worry Be Happy
- Nithyananda Vol. 1
- Instant Tools for Blissful Living
- You Can Heal
- Follow Me In!
- The Door to Enlightenment
- Songs of Eternity
- You are No Sinner
- So You Want to Know The Truth?
- Uncommon answers to Common Questions
- Meditation is for you
- Rising in love with the Master
- Bhagavad Gita Series
- Nithya Yoga - The ultimate practice for body, mind and being
- Open the door...Let the breeze in!

Over 500 FREE discourses of Nithyananda available at http://www.youtube.com/lifeblissfoundation